# THE HISTORIC CITY OF
# NARA
## AN ARCHAEOLOGICAL APPROACH

Exclusively Distributed by:

UNIPUB
4611-F Assembly Drive.
Lanham, MD 20705-4391
301-459-7666

Price: $35.00 plus postage
Order No. U6275

*Authors*

TSUBOI Kiyotari   *b.* 1921

Graduated in 1948 from the Department of History (Archaeology), Kyoto University. Chairman, Japanese National Commission for ICOMOS; Director-General, Osaka Cultural Properties Centre. Former Director-General, Nara National Cultural Properties Research Institute.

TANAKA Migaku   *b.* 1933

M.A., History (Archaeology), Kyoto University. Director, Centre for Archaeological Operations, Nara National Cultural Properties Research Institute.


*Translators*

David W. HUGHES   *b.* 1945

Ph.D. (1985), Anthropology/Music, University of Michigan. Lecturer in Ethnomusicology and Chairman, Centre of Music Studies, School of Oriental and African Studies, University of London.

Gina L. BARNES   *b.* 1947

Ph.D. (1983), Anthropology/Archaeology, University of Michigan. Affiliated Lecturer in East Asian Archaeology, Cambridge University; Senior Researcher, St. John's College, Cambridge.

*Title page*

Looking east from the North Palace Garden Mansion. Viewing the garden from the central buildings of this mansion, the eastern range of mountains of the Nara Basin can be seen in the background. Was this perhaps the inspiration for the later method of constructing landscapes 'borrowed' from nature in Japanese gardens?

*Cover and title page design by Margaret Ng*

# The Historic City of Nara
## An Archaeological Approach

Tsuboi Kiyotari and Tanaka Migaku
Translated by David W. Hughes and Gina L. Barnes

The Centre for East Asian Cultural Studies

First published 1991 by
The United Nations Educational, Scientific and Cultural Organization
7 Place de Fontenoy, 75700 Paris, France
*and*
The Centre for East Asian Cultural Studies
c/o The Toyo Bunko, Honkomagome 2-chome 28-21
Bunkyo-ku, Tokyo 113, Japan
© The Centre for East Asian Cultural Studies/UNESCO 1991

ISBN 92-3-102627-5 (UNESCO)
ISBN 4-89656-501-0 (CEACS)

Printed in Japan by
Komiyama Printing Co., Ltd.

# Contents

# List of Illustrations

## Figures

(*Chapter 3:  Writing, Wooden Tablets, and Ceramics*)

(*Chapter 4:  Ancient Cities, Their Residents, and Urban Life*)

## Plates

# Foreword

The UNESCO programme for the study of historic cities in Asia was launched in 1979. Many of these cities arose, developed and died, while others have survived until today as centres of political, economic, cultural, or religious activity. Some gave birth to satellite cities which grew and complemented each other and the mother city or even outgrew it. Others have been reborn as modern cities or as centres of historical, educational, or cultural tourism with the emphasis on the historical and cultural aspects.

The principal aim of the programme is to contribute to an increased knowledge of various trends in the development and exchange of Asian cultures by studying those cities that have played a significant role in this. The present series is expected to enrich our knowledge of the role of these cities, the typology of their creation and development as well as the transmission of many different cultures throughout the history of Asia.

This book on Nara, the historic city of Japan, is the second in the series. Nara was the Japanese capital from A.D. 710 to 784. It differed essentially from the other great cities of the period in that it was not surrounded by defensive fortifications as were the principal cities in other areas of Asia and other regions of the world.

Since the Nara period was characterized by state-supported Buddhism, there were state-managed Buddhist temples within the capital. Even after the capital was moved north to the present-day city of Kyoto, the old capital of Nara remained the city of the two great Buddhist temples, Kōfukuji and Tōdaiji, the latter housing the world's largest gilt bronze figure of a Buddha. In the course of time, Nara grew into a centre of religious art and commerce. Later, following the Meiji Restoration in 1868, it became the seat of local government for the newly-established Nara Prefecture.

This book narrates the story of Nara as told through the archaeological excavations that have been carried out since 1959 by the Nara National Cultural Properties Research Institute.

The authors are responsible for the choice and presentation of the facts contained in this book and for the opinions expressed therein, which are not necessarily those of UNESCO and do not commit the Organization.

# Preface

Since 1959 there has been almost continuous excavation at the site of Nara Capital, the hub of the ancient Japanese state during the eighth century, and particularly at Nara Palace in the capital's northern sector. These investigations have for the most part been conducted under the direction of the Nara National Cultural Properties Research Institute (colloquially known as Nabunken) and the Nara Municipal Board of Education. The total land area excavated to date has reached 65 hectares.

Only a handful of large-scale Japanese archaeological sites of any period have been excavated systematically and continuously during these same thirty years. These excavations continue to yield results today. Even the most thorough and enduring Japanese excavations pale by comparison with Pompeii, which has been under investigation for more than two centuries. On the other hand, it is gratifying to know that Japanese archaeology, with its modern history of a mere hundred years, has finally reached the point where it can aspire to such lengthy and extensive excavations. In this respect, the Nara Capital excavation has been the pioneer.

Nara, Japan's ancient capital, differed from the other great cities of the ancient world in one important way: it was not surrounded by significant defensive structures. There appears to have been nothing more than a quite unimpressive fence, which has left few traces in the archaeological record, while the principal cities of China, Korea, the rest of Asia, and Europe all began with the erection of impressive walls to protect them from invasion by external enemies. This non-military aspect characterizes not only Nara Capital but the other cities of ancient Japan as well.

The excavations at the Nara site have not only clarified the nature of Nara Capital itself, but have also provided an abundance of information about ancient Japan as a whole. (For the precise meaning of 'ancient Japan' as used in this book, see Chronology in Translators' Note.)

To summarize all the results of the Nara Capital investigation in one book would be wellnigh impossible. It is possible, however, to single out certain turning points in the history of the investigation. These include, for example, the particular incidents of excavation that led to the overturning of a long-cherished theory concerning the extent of Nara Palace (detailed in Chapter 1) and the discovery of the first of the ink-inscribed wooden tablets known as *mokkan* (detailed in Chapter 3). Looking back on them now, it is clear that each of these turning points led to new ideas about the methodology for proper research and excavation. Focusing on several of these turning points and new ideas, we shall describe the broad currents in the investigations at Nara Capital. In so doing, we will be able to introduce not only the major research results, but also several aspects of archaeological practice in Japan. It is hoped that this will appeal to general readers interested in ancient Japan as well as to specialists.

The authors have been involved with Nabunken since the beginning of the excavations, when there was a mere handful of investigators. The excavations under Nabunken's care now occupy thirty-nine full-time researchers. If one includes those who are not directly involved in excavation, the total number of research staff of Nabunken comes to fifty-five. The Nara National Cultural Properties Research Institute has received assistance and moral support from researchers throughout Japan and indeed from other countries. The fact that the excavations at Nara Capital have borne such continual fruit is due in no small part to such outside support.

Several years ago, UNESCO and The Centre for East Asian Cultural Studies suggested to the senior author (Tsuboi) that he might summarize the results of archaeological research at Nara Capital for a foreign readership. Due to other commitments, it was not possible to accomplish this task immediately. Concerned that delays in completing the manuscript would cause considerable inconvenience, Tsuboi consulted with Tanaka. It was decided that Tanaka would draw on a Japanese-language book (*Kodai Nihon o horu* [Excavating ancient Japan], vol. 3, *Heijō-kyō* [Nara Capital]. Tokyo: Iwanami Shoten, 1984) which he had already written on the topic, while incorporating Tsuboi's comments and insights, revising and updating the earlier book extensively, and also casting it in a form more approachable by a non-Japanese audience. Thus was the present book completed.

Each year in Japan sees the completion of thousands of 'rescue excavations' conducted one step ahead of the developers. The ever-increasing flow of information from such excavations has yielded impressive research results. Alas, the language barrier has prevented these results from reaching a wide international audience. It is hoped that the present book, published by UNESCO and CEACS in the interests of international understanding, will go some way towards breaching that barrier.

The text of this book was prepared and submitted to UNESCO in March 1986. Since then many archaeological discoveries have been made at the Nara Capital and Palace sites. These new data, however, have in no way significantly affected or changed our basic understanding of the sites outlined in the pages that follow.

TSUBOI Kiyotari
TANAKA Migaku

October 1990

# Acknowledgements

We would like to extend our gratitude to UNESCO and The Centre for East Asian Cultural Studies, especially to Ikuta Shigeru, the former Chief of the Research and Documentation Section; to the translators, David W. Hughes and Gina L. Barnes (of the Universities of London and Cambridge respectively), for helping to breach the language barrier; to Ozawa Hisashi, who produced the stunning reconstruction drawings; to Matsushima Shūzō, Inoue Kazuo, and others at Iwanami Shoten, publishers of Tanaka's Japanese-language introduction to the Nara Capital excavations, for their cheerful co-operation at every stage of the current venture; to Sawada Masaaki for advice on the section concerning preservation science; to Sahara Makoto and Kitō Kiyoaki for valuable comments on the manuscript as a whole; and to all our colleagues at Nabunken and to many others with whom we have worked in the excavations at Nara Palace and Nara Capital.

Acknowledgements should also be made to Irie Taikichi for providing us with the cover photo, and to the Imperial Repository Shōsōin (fig. 62) and Hōryūji (fig. 22), Kōfukuji (fig. 70, pl. 18), Tōdaiji (cover, figs. 21, 69, pls. 17, 18), and Yakushiji (figs. 67, 68) temples for kindly granting permission to reproduce photographs of their documents, cultural properties, and buildings.

# Translators' Note

The romanization of Japanese terms in the present book follows the modified Hepburn system. The original order of Japanese personal names has been retained, with the family name first.

Virtually all Japanese terms have been rendered into English; exceptions include a few technical terms, such as *mokkan*, which are so widely used and important that the reader should learn them, and a few others where any translation would be confusing or unproductive. The original Japanese expressions are generally shown in the List of Translation Equivalents at the end of the main text.

We present here a table of the names and dates of the major Japanese archaeological and historical periods, many of which are referred to in the text. Beginning and ending dates are approximate and reflect the general consensus.

### Chronology of Japanese History and Prehistory

| PERIOD | DATES |
|---|---|
| *Prehistoric* | |
|     Jōmon | 10000–300 B.C. |
| *Protohistoric* | |
|     Yayoi | 300 B.C.–A.D. 300 |
|     Kofun (Tumulus) | 300–710 |
| *Historic* | |
| Ancient (*kodai*) | |
|     Nara | 710–794 |
|     Heian | 794–1185 |
| Medieval (*chūsei*) | |
|     Kamakura | 1185–1333 |
|     Muromachi | 1333–1573 |
| Early modern (*kinsei*) | |
|     (Azuchi-)Momoyama | 1573–1603 |
|     Tokugawa (Edo) | 1603–1868 |
| Modern (*kindai*) and contemporary (*gendai*) | |
|     Meiji | 1868–1912 |
|     Taishō | 1912–1926 |
|     Shōwa | 1926–1989 |
|     Heisei | 1989–present |

Chapter 1

# Urbanization, Nara Palace, and Its Excavation

## Nara Capital, past and present

Nara was the capital city of Japan in the eighth century. Its nucleus was the Nara Imperial Palace situated at the capital's north-central extremity. In 1967 the question of the Nara Palace site came up for discussion in the Japanese Diet.

*18 April 1967, House of Councillors, Committee on Culture and Education:*
    MEMBER KOBAYASHI TAKESHI: I would particularly like to make a representation to the chairman as well as the Minister of Education. Concerning the Nara Palace question . . . , as a result of investigation, it now seems certain that Nara Capital's East 1st Column Avenue does not run quite as expected but actually bends off on a separate course, so that the site is different from the hypotheses based on early written sources. . . . When I go to call on the Committee for the Protection of Cultural Properties, I would like to request a detailed explanation on this one point.

*22 June 1967, same committee:*
    MEMBER KOBAYASHI: About this bypass, a question has come up. . . . Through excavation of an area next to the Nara Palace remains, by East 1st Column Avenue, an unexpected new situation has arisen, as you know. I'd like some clarification on this point.
    MURAYAMA MATSUO, CHIEF SECRETARY, COMMITTEE FOR THE PROTECTION OF CULTURAL PROPERTIES (precursor of the present Department for the Protection of Cultural Properties in the Agency for Cultural Affairs): The matter of the National Route 24 bypass first came up around 1964. . . . A year or so ago it was decided that, if the bypass had to pass near the Nara Palace remains . . . , the old East 1st Column Avenue along the palace's eastern edge was an important ancient road, so by putting the new bypass there, damage to the site could be kept to a minimum. So the construction plan for the bypass was fundamentally accepted, and we began investigations along the proposed route. The investigations suggested . . . that at a certain time this East 1st Column Avenue might have been used for something besides a road. . . . Nara Palace itself . . . may possibly have spread beyond what is thought to be its original boundary and extended further eastward. . . . As for the bypass, the

present situation is that we have not yet definitely decided to change the plan, but investigations will continue, and if a bypass is still to be built, shouldn't we think about which spot would be the least harmful?

KOBAYASHI: . . . As for the Ministry of Construction . . . , what are your thoughts about the Nara Palace bypass question?

MINOWA KENJIRŌ, CHIEF, ROAD BUREAU, MINISTRY OF CONSTRUCTION: . . . After considering all the proposals, we feel that the route as presently proposed would be the best . . . , and we have decided to go ahead with the bypass. Our present thinking is that we definitely want to be permitted to proceed with this plan.

*20 July 1967, House of Councillors, Committee on Construction:*

MEMBER ŌMORI HISASHI: In the case of the Nara bypass, it's already been decided to proceed with construction. So . . . I'd like to know why the Ministry of Construction is still hesitating.

MINOWA: . . . Excavations have led to the supposition that the eastern edge of Nara Palace is not where it was first thought to be, and that the palace may have extended further to the east. . . . We feel that no route other than the proposed one would serve to alleviate the traffic problem, so we would like to get together with the Committee for the Protection of Cultural Properties and get on with the plans as soon as possible.

The present-day city of Nara lies roughly at the geographical centre of the Japanese islands. The Nara Palace site is situated in the western part of the present-day Nara City limits. To the west is Osaka, Japan's third largest city (pop. 2.54 million); to the north, Kyoto, the seventh largest city (pop. 1.42 million); both are thirty minutes away by private railway (see map in endpapers). If you get off at Saidaiji Station and walk ten minutes to the east, you will come to the Nara Palace site.

The road from the station runs through the heart of Nara's western shopping district. The neighbourhood of the palace site is also filling up steadily with houses. In 1959, when excavations at the Nara Palace site began in earnest, little besides rice paddies and vegetable gardens lay between the station and the site. The intervening thirty years have seen considerable change (fig. 1). During that period the population of Nara has more than doubled, from 130,000 to 344,000. Lying in the commuter belt of the two large cities mentioned above, the Nara Palace site faces the threat of destruction through modern urbanization. It was in such a context that the preceding discussions took place in the Diet.

The discussions stemmed from plans to build a bypass for National Route 24 linking Kyoto and Nara. Crossing the hills separating Kyoto and Nara Prefectures, Route 24 proceeded southward, grazing the western edge of Tōdaiji, a Buddhist temple founded in the eighth century. Route 24 turned west by another eighth-century temple, Kōfukuji, cutting through modern Nara's central district before continuing further south into the Nara Basin. Only 6 metres wide, the highway was unable to cope with the wave of 'motorization' which had surged over the country since the late 1950s. Bottlenecks and congestion increased. Inevitably, plans were made for the construction of a highway to connect Kyoto and the central

**1** The conditions of excavation around the Nara Palace site. *Top:* the Nara Palace site surrounded by fields, 1948; *bottom:* the Nara Palace site as an island of green within a residential district, 1984.

Nara Basin directly, bypassing old Nara proper. The plan also called for the reconstruction and utilization of the ancient road system of Nara Capital. In the course of archaeological excavation, however, it became clear that the regular grid layout of the roads had been disrupted in one spot. What should have been a road adjacent to the palace was apparently part of the palace itself. If the original bypass plans were followed, the palace site would be sliced in two. In reaction to this, a nationwide citizens' movement demanded the total preservation of the Nara Palace site, and its voice was heard even in the Diet.

The Palaeolithic in Japan yielded to the hunting and gathering culture known as the Jōmon, which lasted some 10,000 years. Wet rice agriculture reached the Japanese archipelago in the late fourth century B.C., marking the beginning of the Yayoi period. By the mid-third century A.D., large mounded tombs (kofun) had begun to appear throughout the land, giving their name to the Kofun (Tumulus) period. These tumuli were the overt signs of the emergence of powerful regional rulers. Buddhism entered from the continent during the sixth century. In the seventh century, much of Japan was united under the first centralized state, with its centre in Yamato—the ancient name for what is now Nara Prefecture.* At the apex of the pyramid of power stood the emperor. The first geographical centre of power was located in the Asuka district in southern Yamato, focusing on the emperor's residence. This residence was called the *miya*—'honourable house'. Gradually, government and administrative offices grew up around the residence, eventually coalescing with it to form a compound of a much larger scale. In English, such a compound would usually be called 'a palace'; in Japanese, the term used is still *miya*. (Incidentally, *miya* also refers to a Shinto shrine, which is of course also an 'honourable house' for a deity or spirit.)

In 694 Empress Jitō moved to nearby Fujiwara. It is here that we find the first definite evidence of a regular grid pattern of streets, laid out around the palace according to Chinese models. This became the standard layout for ancient Japanese imperial capitals. In 710 the capital moved from Fujiwara to Nara where it remained until 784, except for the years 740–45, when it was moved briefly to three other locations (Kuni, Shigaraki, and Naniwa). Relocated to Nagaoka in 784, the imperial capital finally settled down in Heian ten years later in 794. Heian Capital —later renamed Kyoto—remained the emperor's seat until the move to Tokyo in 1868.

During the eighth century, the Korean Peninsula was under the control of the Silla kings; in China, the Tang empire was at its peak. The Saracen empire which arose on the Arabian Peninsula clashed with the Tang to the east and took control

---

*With the establishment of a centralized state, pre-existing territorial divisions were regularized into an administrative system divided into *kuni* ('provinces') and again into *kōri* or *gun* ('counties'). The number of these units changed from time to time. For example, there were fifty-eight *kuni* in the early eighth century, sixty-six in the early ninth century; and the 550 *kōri* of the eighth century had grown to 631 by the eighteenth century. At the time of the Meiji Restoration in 1868 the *kuni-kōri* system was replaced by the modern prefectural system. Modern Nara Prefecture corresponds to the earlier Yamato Province, which contained Nara Capital as well as 15 counties. Osaka Prefecture has incorporated three of these provinces: Kawachi, Izumi, and half of Settsu; this territory comprised 25 counties during the eighth century.

of Spain to the west; their spread into the rest of Europe was blocked by the Byzantine empire and by the Franks under Charlemagne. This was the age of Nara Capital.

Up to now we have been using the terms Nara Palace and Nara Capital. In modern Japanese, Nara Palace is usually called Heijō-kyū and Nara Capital is called Heijō-kyō. *Kyū* means 'palace' and is written with the Chinese character 宮; *kyō* means 'capital' and is written 京. Encountering the term *kyō* today, one thinks of those ancient quasi-urban capitals which are laid out symmetrically around a north-south axis, with their streets crossing at right angles like a chessboard whose pieces are shrines and temples, houses of nobles and officials, public market places, etc.—all disposed according to a careful plan. In these ancient capitals, the central north-south axis was named Scarlet Phoenix Avenue; the region east of this axis was called the Left Capital, and to the west lay the Right Capital. In Nara Capital, these two regions formed a rectangle measuring 4.8 kilometres north to south and 4.3 kilometres east to west, while east of the Left Capital was a rectangular projection, 2.1 kilometres north to south and 1.6 kilometres east to west, which is today called the Outer Capital. At the northern end of Scarlet Phoenix Avenue lay Nara Palace (fig. 2). The palace occupied an area 1.1 kilometres square with an eastern projection of 0.8 × 0.3 kilometres. Besides the Imperial Domicile, the palace included a Great Supreme Hall; a State Halls Compound for state ceremonials, official negotiations, and the like; and various offices, bureaux, and workshops.*

During the eighth century Heijō-kyō and Heijō-kyū were called Nara-no-miyako and Nara-no-miya respectively, although the former terms are more commonly heard today. The confusion of terms results from the borrowing of the Chinese writing system to express the genetically unrelated Japanese language. Chinese characters (*kanji*, as they are called in Japanese) are largely ideographic, so that pronunciation is not directly specified. A typical *kanji* will be given several readings in Japanese, depending on context. 'Heijō', for example, is written with two characters: 平, meaning 'flat' or 'level', read (among others) *hei*, *hyō*, and *taira;* and 城 ('castle' or 'fortress'), which may be read *sei* (with variant *zei*), *jō*, and *shiro*. *Hyō* and *jō* represent the Japanese attempt to imitate the pronunciation these characters were given in southern China around the fourth and fifth centuries; the Japanized pronunciations of this period are called '*go* 呉 readings'. *Hei* and *sei/zei* represent the Japanized pronunciations of the north Chinese standard language of the seventh and eighth centuries. Such sounds are called '*kan* 漢 readings'. *Taira* and *shiro* are indigenous Japanese words felt to be synonymous with these Chinese words and are thus written with these same characters, although their pronunciations are totally different.

In modern Japanese, it is not uncommon to mix *go* readings, *kan* readings, and/or Japanese pronunciations in a single word, Heijō being one example. During the eighth and ninth centuries, however, such commingling was rare. If we assume that 平城 was read with a Japanized Chinese pronunciation during the eighth

---

*Further details of the layout of the capital, including the principles behind the naming of blocks and streets, will be found in the opening pages of Chapter 4.

century, it should have been either Heizei or Hyōjō. Actually, though, there is no evidence that these characters, when followed by 京 or 宮, were read in Chinese style at all. The Chinese-style readings for these latter characters are *kyō* and *kyū* as in Heijō-kyō and Heijō-kyū. But as we have seen above, they also have Japanese readings, *miyako* and *miya*. The three-character compounds 平城京 and 平城宮 were, it appears, not read *Heijō-kyō* and *Heijō-kyū* at all, but instead were read *Nara-no-miyako* and *Nara-no-miya*. Why the name Nara came to be written with the characters 平城 is not well understood; the etymology of the name Nara itself is still subject to debate. In any case, we adhere to the ancient pronunciation: *Nara*. Incidentally, in modern Japanese the place-name Nara is written with two other Chinese characters, 奈良, used purely for their phonetic value, in rebus fashion.

## The rise of the eight-*chō*-square theory

In 1959, the year in which the Nara Palace excavations began in earnest, two points regarding the palace were taken for granted: its date and its location. The capital was assumed to have been moved from Fujiwara in 710, four years after the accession of Empress Genmei, and was relocated to Nagaoka in 784, the fourth year of Kanmu's reign. This capital was a square plot of land measuring 8 *chō* on a side,* straddling the boundary between Saki-chō and Nijō-chō, two districts of modern Nara City, in the northern part of the Nara Basin.

The fact that Nara was the capital from 710 to 784 is clear from the *Shoku Nihongi*.** However, the earliest source for the size and plan of Nara Palace itself is a seventeenth-century document. In 1681 the poet Hayashi Sōho, who lived near the palace site, published a twenty-volume work describing ancient sites in the Yamato region (*Washū kyūseki yūkō*). Around that time, presumably because the custom of making pilgrimages to a series of famous shrines and temples had begun to spread from the nobility to the commoners, there appeared several woodblock-printed guidebooks to Yamato, a province rich in historic religious sites. Hayashi's gazetteer was one of the earliest of these guidebooks, covering in detail the fifteen counties of Yamato. Hayashi not only included existing shrines and temples, he also visited, investigated and reported on sites that had long since vanished under

---

*In 1959 Japan officially adopted the metric system and abandoned the earlier system of measurement. This earlier system, which is still used in certain special circumstances, had its origins in Chinese practices imported during the sixth century and was officially adopted in Japan in the seventh century. Undergoing slight modifications, it survived unchallenged until the metric system was made a legal alternative in 1891. The unit of length called the *shaku*, although approximating the Western 'foot', varied somewhat in different eras. Archaeological evidence shows that the *shaku* hovered around 29.7 cm during the eighth century. Over the centuries, however, it gradually lengthened until it was fixed as 30.3 cm in the nineteenth century. A *shaku* contains 10 *sun* or 100 *bu;* there are 10 *shaku* in a *jō* but 6 *shaku* in a *ken*. 1 *chō* = 60 *ken* = 360 *shaku* = ca. 109 metres. The length of a city block in Heian Capital was also called one *chō;* but in that case the distance in question was approximately 130 metres. The same term could indicate surface area as well as length, as we shall see in Chapter 4.

**The *Shoku Nihongi* (*Continued Chronicle of Japan*), completed in the year 797, covers events of importance to the court from the year 697 to 791. Unlike the two earlier 'chronicles', the *Kojiki* (*Record of Ancient Matters*) and *Nihongi* or *Nihonshoki* (*Chronicle of Japan*), it is considered highly reliable in terms of historical accuracy.

agricultural land. In all, it must be adjudged a superb geography for its time. In volume 5 we read, 'Nara Palace: The palace's eastern half is in Sōnokami county and its western half is in Sōnoshimo county. . . . Its remains are in the Nijō area of Chōshōji village and are 8 *chō* on a side.' The place-name Nijō survives as the modern district of Nijō-chō, in which the western half of the palace site lies. Hayashi thus provides us with an early impression of the size, plan, and location of the palace.

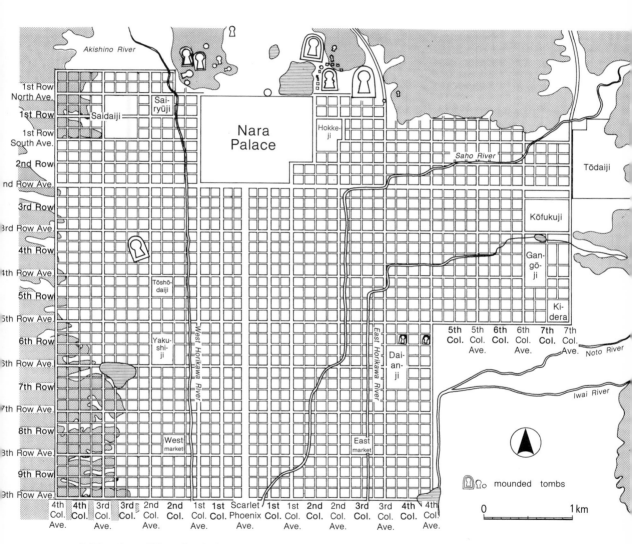

**2** The plan of Nara Capital and Nara Palace. Nara Capital was constructed in A.D. 710 in the northern Nara Basin, based on the model of the ancient Chinese gridded city plan. At the north central edge of the capital stood Nara Palace, seat of political activity and home of the imperial family.

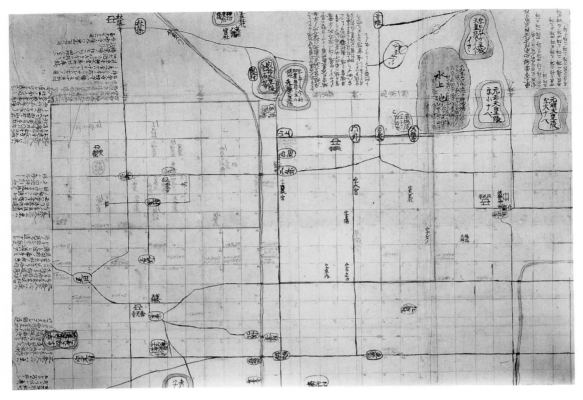

3 The street map of Nara Capital drawn by Kitaura Sadamasa. Using evidence from archaeological remains such as burial mounds and temples, from place-names, and from the layout of fields, Kitaura reconstructed the street plan of Nara Capital. This was the first investigation of the Nara Capital site.

In the nineteenth century Kitaura Sadamasa (1817–71) conducted the first thorough investigation of the capital, resulting in his reconstructed map of Nara Capital (fig. 3). To supplement his own observations he consulted two other documents: a map of the Right Capital (i.e., the western half of Nara Capital), preserved in Saidaiji temple not far from the palace site; and a map of Heian Capital (modern Kyoto) included in the *Shūkai-shō*, a fourteenth-century volume of articles on ceremonies, customs, etc. Comparing the Nara and Heian Capitals, Kitaura reached two conclusions: that their overall plans were quite similar; but that Heian Palace was 10 *chō* north to south by 8 *chō* east to west, while the evidence of place-names and topography suggested that Nara Palace was 8 *chō* square.

Kitaura was born in Furuichi village, Sōnokami county, Yamato Province (modern Furuichi-chō, Nara City). For several generations his family had worked for the Tōdō clan in the administrative offices of Yamato fief. The Tōdō were based in neighbouring Ise Province, modern Mie Prefecture. Sadamasa himself was employed there in a relatively minor capacity from the age of fifteen. His free time was devoted to research on such topics as imperial mausolea, the ancient agricultural system of the Nara Basin, the layout of Nara Capital, place-names, and what we would now call historical geography. The Tokugawa shogunate found his research particularly useful in carrying out the maintenance and repair of imperial tombs; this was presumably the reason for his official elevation to samurai status in 1863.

With the Meiji Restoration of 1868, Japan took a major step along the road to becoming a modern state. During the Meiji era, Kitaura's research provided a base for Sekino Tadashi (1867–1935) to conduct further on-site investigations and make his own contribution to the scholarly debate over Nara Capital. Sekino graduated from the College of Engineering, Tokyo Imperial University, with a specialization in architecture, and in 1895 he was appointed director for the repair of old shrines and temples in Nara Prefecture. Thus began his involvement with Nara Capital. He kept a diary of developments, according to which in December 1898 he made plans to study the capital and began to purchase reference books. In January 1899 he discovered the apparent remains of the palace's Great Supreme Hall and other structures, and by February he had completed a scale map of the topography of the palace site. In October he completed his manuscript *Observations on the Remains of the Great Supreme Hall in Nara Palace*. His work soon began to reach the public eye through newspaper articles. In 1901 he left Nara to return to his old university as an associate professor. His researches finally appeared in their fullest form in 1907, when *Considerations on Nara Capital and the Greater Palace Enclosure* was published as volume 3 of the *Bulletin of the College of Engineering, Tokyo Imperial University*. Sekino's impressive legacy of subsequent publications centred on architectural history but also extended to archaeology, aesthetic history, and other fields. His investigations were not confined to Japan but took him to Korea and China as well.

Sekino's theories formed the basis for the work of later researchers of Nara Capital, and he shared the opinion of his predecessors that the palace had been 8 *chō* square: 'The palace lay in the north-central part of the capital . . . , bordered on the south by 2nd Row Avenue, on east and west by the respective 1st Column Avenues of the Left and Right Capitals, and on the north by 1st Row North Avenue. It measured 8 *chō* east to west and 8 *chō* south to north.'

We do not know when the idea that the palace measured 8 *chō* on a side first came into existence. Hayashi Sōho is the earliest known proponent, but it is unclear whether his claim was based on field investigation or merely on hearsay evidence. Kitaura Sadamasa used a special measuring wagon (converted from a freight cart) and took on-site measurements. The place-names on which he relied are recorded in his reconstructed map of Nara Capital: within the palace grounds are shown such names as Daikokuden (Great Supreme Hall), Ōmiya (Grand Palace), Baba (Riding Ground), and Dairi-no-miya (Inner Palace). These are all names evocative of a palace site and all survive to this day as local place-names.

To those familiar with Japanese archaeology, this discussion may recall the existence of several sites located in places named Hōhatchō ('eight *chō* square'). These are most numerous in the Tōhoku region of northern Honshū. One theory is that Hōhatchō marks the former presence of a seat of provincial government or similar complex. Another is that the name indicates a particular type of ancient frontier settlement. Excavations began at one such site in 1976, Hōhatchō site, Ōta, Morioka City, Iwate Prefecture. It is now clear that the site was an ancient administrative centre nearly 1 kilometre square. Current opinion holds it to be the site of Shiwa Castle, built in 803 as one of the important bases for controlling the northern frontier. In the same prefecture, in the Sakuragawa section of Mizusawa City, the remains of Isawa Castle also lie in a neighbourhood called Hōhatchō. This castle was built in 802 to be the principal military centre for the subjugation of the Emishi— the name by which the central government designated the residents of northern Japan who resisted the expansion of its control. Excavations at Isawa Castle in 1954–55 revealed traces of buildings. They also exposed earthworks which interestingly enough limit the site's area to about 650 metres per side, or about 6 *chō*. Despite discrepancies in actual size, these two sites clearly point to a connection between the name Hōhatchō and ancient administrative centres. However, we are still not justified in assuming that *all* places with this name will show such a connection. In some cases, the name might merely have been borrowed from such a centre.

The name Hōhatchō, or other place-names containing the element *hatchō* ('eight *chō*'), do occur, if rarely, outside the Tōhoku region. The name Doi-hatchō has since the medieval period been associated with an area in modern Hōfu City, Yamaguchi Prefecture. This is known to have been the site of the government offices of Suō Province. According to some scholars, the name Hōhatchō in Fukayasu county, Hiroshima Prefecture, indicates the former government seat of Bingo Province, but the connection is uncertain. The place-name Kuni-hatchō appears in a manorial illustration from the fourteenth or fifteenth century, and the location in question can be linked with the government seat of Tamba Province.

Therefore, although we may be uncertain about the date of origin of this term and the precise degree to which it is linked with the size and function of a site, there is a strong likelihood of its having spread widely through its association with public facilities for local governance. The expression *hatchō-shihō* ('eight *chō* square'), meaning an extraordinarily splendid private mansion and grounds, may stem from such origins. For example, the term *hatchō-shihō* appears in the sacred writings of Tenri-kyō, a 'new religion' born in Nara Prefecture in the mid-nineteenth century; also, in a volume of quotations from the Tenri-kyō foundress, we find the sentence, 'The estate is eight *chō* square.' Tenri-kyō has decreed as sacred ground an area eight *chō* square centred on the foundress's former residence, and the church's headquarters are being built there. The foundress was the wife of a bankrupt rural landlord; it is interesting that the concept and the expression 'eight *chō* square' should have been so widely disseminated as to occur even in the speech of this relatively humble woman.

Such is the historical background of the designation of Nara Palace as 'eight *chō* square'.

### Excavations at Nara Palace

Research on Nara Palace and Nara Capital is at present being conducted principally under the auspices of the Nara National Cultural Properties Research Institute (abbreviation, Nabunken). Established in 1952, Nabunken works in co-operation with the Boards of Education for both Nara Prefecture and Nara City. Its purpose is to conduct research into all aspects of Japan's cultural heritage—arts and crafts, architecture, history, etc.—chiefly on the basis of the actual remains of ancient cultural properties which occur so abundantly in Nara. Nabunken's involvement with Nara Palace began at the end of 1953.

The post-war occupation of Japan by the Allied Forces had just ended. Adjacent to the northwest corner of old Nara City proper—the northeast corner of the palace site—there was an Allied military base. South of the base, there was a road running east to west, known to the local residents as 1st Row Road (Ichijō-dōri). Barely able to accommodate an oxcart, 1st Row Road was selected for upgrading and widening to improve the flow of traffic between the military base and Osaka. The work began in 1953. At the point where the road crossed the palace site, some archaeological features were discovered. The prefectural Board of Education carried out emergency excavations at the end of the year, with the result that a nationally administered investigation was begun in January 1954 by the Committee for the Protection of Cultural Properties. This was the first post-war investigation within the site of Nara Capital. It was undertaken, not because of an expressed need to clarify particular questions of scholarly interest concerning the palace or the capital, but merely because road construction had led to digging in the area, a set of circumstances which may be considered typical of post-war archaeological investigation in Japan. Nabunken participated in the Nara Palace excavations as the only national research organ in the region.

Subsequently, Nabunken became involved in further excavations in the region, with the intention of providing data to guide the formulation of policies to cope with ever more numerous development projects. During the three years following the first survey of the site in 1955, archaeologists tended to concentrate their efforts on surveying Asuka in the southern Nara Basin; but since 1959 the Nara Palace site has been under continuous excavation. In the thirty years since, the area excavated in more than 200 separate investigations has totalled 35 hectares—about 27 per cent of the entire palace site (fig. 4). Investigations in recent years have tended to move out beyond the palace boundary, so that digging is now in progress throughout the capital.

Since Nabunken began research on the palace, the current state of the site has been well documented through such means as aerial photography and the preparation of 1:1,000 scale topographical maps. For a long while there was nothing to cast doubt on the eight-*chō*-square theory of the palace. In aerial photographs, the former layout of the streets of the old capital is clearly reflected in the long narrow paddies and vegetable gardens: 2nd Row Avenue, passing east to west just south of the palace; West 1st Column Avenue on its western edge; East 1st Column Avenue, supposedly forming its eastern border (fig. 5). What Kitaura and Sekino had noticed on the ground was examined from the air for the first time, and little was found to object to in their conclusions. This is perhaps not surprising, considering that all conclusions were based on the same methodology, that is, observation of the present-day surface topography of the site. Only a new methodology could significantly challenge the *status quo*, and the obvious one was actual excavation. In 1963 a series of excavations, aimed at ascertaining the palace boundaries, was

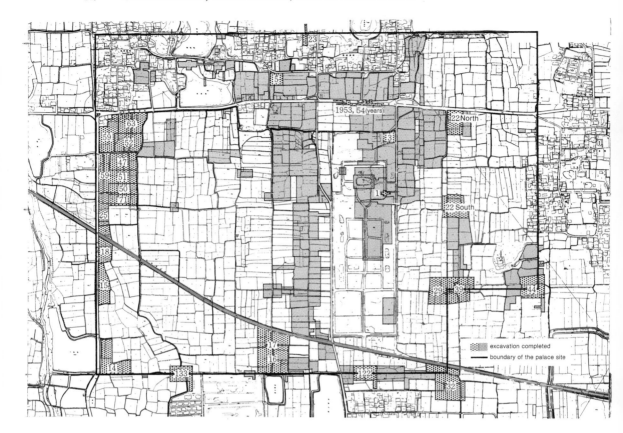

4  Locations of Nara Palace excavations. Since gaining momentum in the 1950s, excavation of
Nara Palace has extended to 27% of the site's area. The numbered locations are excavation
numbers utilized in this book.

begun. It was these excavations which led to the negation of the eight-*chō*-square
theory. The first excavation was conducted in what was thought to be the southwestern corner of the palace grounds. In terms of Nabunken's palace excavations,
this was Excavation No. 14.

In typological terms, Nara Palace was a 'triple-nested compound', that is, a set
of three fences or walls enclosing progressively more of the grounds. The innermost
fence surrounded only the Imperial Domicile, scene of the emperor's daily activities. The second fence enclosed the first fence as well as the bureaux (i.e., offices
and workshops) of those responsible for attending to the personal needs of the imperial family. The outermost wall enclosed all of this and also the bureaux of public
administration and government, and therefore the entire palace precincts. In each
of the three walls stood several gates; the gates in each successive wall were known
collectively as the Inner, Middle, and Outer Gates. The outermost wall was called
the Palace Wall or, since it was the largest, the Great Palace Compound Wall, or
simply the Great Wall.

The gates of the two inner walls were provided with registers of the names of

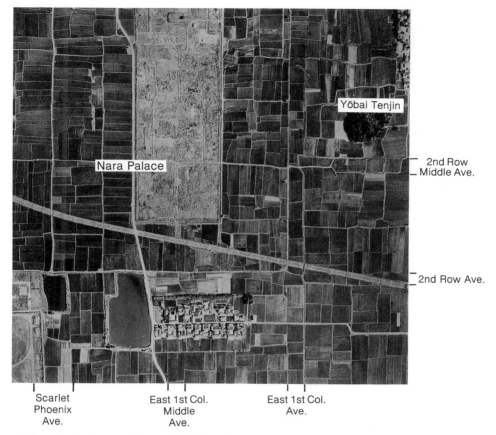

Yōbai Tenjin

Nara Palace

2nd Row Middle Ave.

2nd Row Ave.

Scarlet Phoenix Ave.

East 1st Col. Middle Ave.

East 1st Col. Ave.

5 Nara Capital street plan as visible in the modern paddy-field layout. Nara Palace is at top centre.

those persons permitted entrance. Visitors would state their names before the gate and await confirmation before passing through. In this way access to the two inner enclosures was strictly regulated. There seems, however, to have been no such register for the Outer Gates. Does this suggest that there were fewer restrictions on access to the government bureaux?

Excavation No. 14 succeeded in determining the location of the western end of the southern segment of the Great Wall. The nature of the wall's construction was also revealed. First, a trench was dug, 8.5 metres wide and about 1 metre deep, then a layer of clay was laid as a foundation. Finally, earth of good quality was piled up and tamped down firmly to form the wall itself. At ground level the Great Wall was 2.7 metres thick. Above ground, however, only a small portion of the lower section survives. Excavation along the extrapolated line marking the southern boundary turned up a large quantity of roof tiles, making it clear that the top of the wall was tiled.

This information about the Great Wall at the palace's southern boundary also led to doubts about previous research approaches to early capital sites. The Great

Wall's basal width was 2.7 metres (9 *shaku*), and the distance between the wall and its outer moat was 10.5 metres (35 *shaku*). By contrast, the Engi Shiki (Procedures of the Engi Era), a collection of laws and by-laws published in the early tenth century, notes that the Great Wall of the later Heian Palace was 7 *shaku* thick and stood 25.5 *shaku* from the moat. Thus the scale of Nara Palace's outer defences seems to have been somewhat more grandiose than the Heian capital's.

Prior to full-scale excavation, assumptions concerning the layout and structure of the Nara Palace buildings rested chiefly on what was known of Heian Palace. Built in 794 after the move from Nagaoka, Heian Palace survived unscathed until 960, but during the next 122 years, fourteen major fires are recorded. Each time the palace was rebuilt or repaired, the intention was to reconstruct the original form of 794. To do this, it was first necessary to clarify that original form and recover the palace's exact dimensions. The research and resulting scale drawings from the tenth and eleventh centuries were in answer to the practical need for accurate reference materials in rebuilding palaces destroyed by fire. We also have access to a rich body of depictions of Heian Palace in picture scrolls and descriptions in contemporary literature. Thus it is possible to feel quite confident in our understanding of even very minute details of the palace's structure.

Virtually no such documentation is available for Nara Palace. It was therefore only natural to rely on information about Heian Palace, although in fact there was no way of knowing to what degree this information was actually applicable to Nara. With excavation, it gradually became apparent that there were both similarities and disparities between the two palaces. For example, we have noted that both have a Great Wall surrounded by a strip of open land and then by a moat, but that there is a difference in their dimensions. We must therefore recognize the limitations in thinking about Nara Palace in terms of Heian Palace.

Since only the base of the Great Wall at Nara survives, we can only guess at its

6 Reconstruction of a portion of the Great Wall surrounding Nara Palace. The Great Wall was 2.7 m thick and probably more than 6 m high.

height. The Engi Shiki state that a wall 6 *shaku* thick shall stand 13 *shaku* tall, while a wall 4 *shaku* thick shall be 8 to 9 *shaku* tall. Extrapolating from these figures, a wall 9 *shaku* thick such as at Nara would have had a height of some 20 *shaku*—about 6 metres. There is now no way to confirm this hypothesis; however, when a portion of the Great Wall was to be 'restored' in 1982, scale drawings were made on the assumption of a thickness of 9 *shaku* and a height of 20 *shaku;* the result, especially if roof tiles were added on top of this, seemed to be slightly too tall and somewhat unbalanced aesthetically. It is no easy matter to reconstruct standing structures solely on the basis of their subsurface remains, so in restoring the wall, it was therefore decided to use the 9-*shaku* thickness revealed by excavation but to limit the height to the largest figure given in the Engi Shiki for such tamped-earth roofed walls. Thus the height for reconstruction was set at 5.6 metres (fig. 6).

Portions of the south Great Wall were first excavated in 1963. Later in that year and in 1965 the west Great Wall was dug, and the north Great Wall in 1964. By 1965, then, three borders of the palace complex had been delimited. They were found to accord with the eight-*chō*-square theory. More detailed data about the south Great Wall were also added by the 1964 excavation of the Scarlet Phoenix Gate, which was the principal entrance for the whole complex, and the unearthing in 1978–79 of the eastern and western gates and their immediate surroundings.

An enormous number of roof tiles were excavated in the vicinity of the Great Wall. The arrangement of the tiles, lined up as if they had just slid off a roof, makes it clear that they had been set on top of the wall. In traditional Japanese architecture each of the tiles along the eaves generally has a design on its edge. Interestingly enough, of the eave tiles excavated along the southern portion of the Great Wall, more than half have designs also found on tiles recovered from the immediately preceding palace at Fujiwara (fig. 7 *left*).

**7** Nara Palace roof-tile designs. During the first stage of palace construction, many tiles were brought from the buildings of Fujiwara Palace (694–710) and reused (*left*); later, tiles were manufactured specifically for Nara Palace (*right*).

At Fujiwara a wide range of different eave-tile designs was found, and several of these occur at Nara. It may be that the eave tiles used at Nara were not manufactured specially for that particular palace but were 'recycled' from Fujiwara Palace. Nara is not the only such case: a similar phenomenon had already been observed at the Nagaoka and Heian Capitals. It appears to have been common to tear down some of the buildings of a capital at the time of its abandonment and to transport the materials for use at the new site. Excavations at Nara to date have shown that Fujiwara-style eave tiles are particularly concentrated along the south Great Wall and around its gates. On the inner palace buildings, however, new tiles with unique designs were used (fig. 7 *right*). Perhaps we can assume the following scenario. There was presumably a desire to complete the south Great Wall, which was the front facade for the entire palace compound, as quickly as possible, along with the palace's central buildings. Such new tiles as could be quickly manufactured were used on the central buildings, but it was necessary to use some lumber and tiles from Fujiwara on the south Great Wall and its gates. The rest of the compound could be completed at a more leisurely pace after the move to Nara, which meant that there was time to manufacture a sufficient quantity of new tiles.

From south to west to north, the boundaries of the palace grounds were gradually revealed through direct observation of the features themselves. The eight-*chō*-square theory, accepted since the time of Hayashi Sōho, seemed to have been confirmed beyond doubt. Then came the Nara Bypass.

### The Nara Bypass and Nara Palace

According to plans drawn up by the Ministry of Construction beginning in 1961, the Nara Bypass was to be 26 metres wide and accommodate 30,000 vehicles per day. It would slice the northern Nara Basin in half along a north-south line. There were three proposals for its location: it would run along the reconstructed path of East 1st, 2nd, or 3rd Column Avenue of the ancient capital (fig. 8). The final choice was East 1st Column Avenue, which had supposedly run along the eastern boundary of Nara Palace. From the Ministry's point of view, this choice had several advantages. Aside from giving the bypass the additional function of separating the palace site from the central district of Nara City, it made sense in terms of city planning, that is, it was in a high-priority location for a new thoroughfare, it would minimize the risk of destroying cultural remains, and it would require almost no relocating of houses. Lastly, it was the most economical option in terms of construction costs.

The Committee for the Protection of Cultural Properties (CPCP) agreed to this plan but attached the following four stipulations:

1. The road should be routed so as to run east of the palace's outer moat rather than overlap it.
2. Care should be taken not to interfere with the preservation of the site, by methods such as the use of overpasses and the maintenance of open space surrounding archaeological features.
3. The CPCP should be consulted as the planning proceeded.

4. Where the existence of archaeological features was suspected, pre-construction excavations should be conducted at the expense of the government contractors.

Thus harmony was achieved between the Ministry of Construction and the CPCP, and the East 1st Column Avenue scheme was launched.

The need for a bypass was generally recognized. Given the considerable awareness of cultural history in Japan, nearly everyone favoured a plan leading to the reconstruction of the street grid of the ancient capital. However, although the course of East 1st Column Avenue could be discerned clearly on the surface from present-day agricultural field patterns, there had as yet been no excavation in search of subsurface features. If the bypass was to lie east of the palace moat, it would first be necessary to find the moat. The archaeologists were in accord: 'There is no choice but to do some pre-construction excavating. Since we have been investigating the other three edges of the palace grounds, we might as well get around to the eastern edge!'

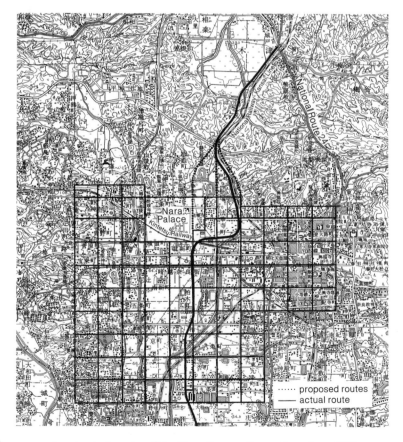

**8** The proposed and actual routes of the Nara Bypass. Excavations from 1964, accompanying the planning of the Nara Bypass, obtained data which thoroughly overturned the 'eight-*chō*-square' theory widely held until that time to account for Nara Palace's shape.

Excavation was to begin at four points: the presumed locations of the three gates of the east Great Wall and the southeast corner. Expenses were borne jointly by the Ministries of Education and Construction; administrative responsibilities fell to the prefectural Board of Education; and the excavations were directed by Nabunken. Investigation started first at the presumed northern and middle east gates, respectively 250 metres and 500 metres south of the presumed point of the northeast corner of the palace grounds. Counting from the first dig in 1955, this was Excavation No. 22; the two simultaneous excavations were referred to as No. 22 North and No. 22 South (see fig. 4).

The first step in an excavation is removal of the topsoil, and this began at Excavation No. 22 North on 30 November 1964. The entire research area of 33 ares consisted of paddy, with a depth some 20 centimetres of cultivated soil. Paddy topsoil is of no real value to the archaeologist, since it rarely contains any artifacts and is so regularly disturbed by ploughing and planting. Once it has been cleared away, the soil below is searched rigorously for artifacts and features, and the location and condition of any finds are recorded carefully. To aid in measurement, wooden surveying posts are driven into the ground. At the Nara Palace site, the entire area was marked off by such posts into sections 3 metres square, which were the minimal units for recording finds. These squares were given four-character addresses in a matrix consisting of two alphabetical characters and a two-digit number. Each of these matrices was further identified as to its location in Nara Palace as a whole, by an address consisting of a number plus three letters. The resulting eight-digit combinations indicate where on the Japanese archipelago each 3-metre-square (9 m$^2$) section is located. Take the address 6AAC PU18, for example. 6AAC identifies an area some 200 metres east to west and 70 metres north to south. This code includes the site of Excavation No. 22 North. PU18 indicates the northwest corner of 6AAC. These local four-character addresses are written directly onto the surveying posts. If you stand at any point on the excavation site and face southeast, the figure on the nearest post in that direction is your address.

The task of removing the dug soil continues. Layers of soil differing in colour and quality lie one atop the other. Items found in the upper strata should be newer, that is, younger than those found further down. What artifacts occur in which strata? Which strata contain traces of building activity? Such important questions pertaining to the *stratigraphy* can be answered only at the excavation site. However, it is no easy task, even for the experienced investigator, to discern minor changes in the nature of the soil; and it is sometimes necessary to be able to re-examine the soil stratigraphy after excavating an area. For that reason, some strips of soil are left unexcavated, criss-crossing the site like the raised paths between rice paddies (see fig. 9 *top left*). At the Nara Palace site, such strips were left every four to five sections; in other words, every 12 to 15 metres. Except for these strips, the entire site is excavated. At this stage the soil is dug with hoes and spades and carried away on a conveyor belt (pl. 3).

Immediately below the topsoil is the so-called 'paddy base'. In most paddies this is an artificial, tamped-earth layer which often contains artifacts from the medieval and early modern periods. Of course, artifacts of the ancient period may also be found. At Excavation No. 22 North, the paddy base was some 20 centimetres thick. Immediately below was a dark brown layer rich in organic matter, containing many artifacts from the Nara period. Within this layer differences in soil quality and colour were, on the whole, so minimal as to elude detection. Below this dark brown layer, that is, some 60 to 70 centimetres below the surface, the excavators began to discover postholes and other evidence of buildings. The first posthole was identified on 24 December 1964, the twenty-fifth day of excavation. Since this discovery was made just as the year was ending, further investigation was postponed until after the New Year holidays.

When excavation resumed in January 1965, many features began to emerge, principally in the southern half of the site. Most immediately noticeable were the numerous postholes for the erection of vertical 'embedded pillars' (fig. 9 *bottom left*). These postholes were about a metre square and a metre deep; within each posthole a round pillar with a diameter of 30 centimetres or so had once been embedded. In most cases, the pillars had been removed or had rotted away. Occasionally a portion of its base remained in the posthole. This portion is called the 'pillar root'. The postholes found in this area were no different from those found in other parts of the palace grounds. Postholes could be detected by slight differences in colour and compactness of the soil which had eventually filled them. When such

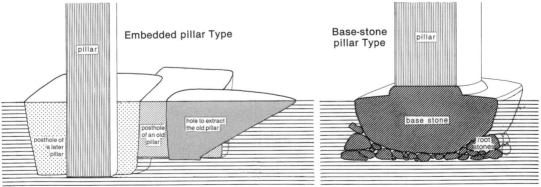

**9** Two types of building. In the Nara period, there were buildings constructed with pillars embedded in the ground (*left*) and those whose pillars rested on base stones (*right*).

**10** Two well locations at the *Sake*-making Bureau. At a location hypothesized to sit astride East 1st Column Avenue, the remains of sizeable wells and buildings were discovered, revealing that this was no avenue but instead lay inside the Nara Palace grounds.

postholes lay at regular intervals in straight lines, the obvious assumption is that they formed part of a building or wall.

Postholes were not the only finds. In late January a ditch was found slightly to the south of the centre of the excavation site. The bottom and sides of the ditch were lined with spherical stones each about the size of a human head. Another ditch demarcated a raised platform some 7.5 metres square, the first such feature found on the palace site. Then at the end of January a well was found in the centre of this platform (fig. 10 *left*). It was enclosed on the surface by a board frame some 2.8 metres square (inner dimensions). A double layer of boards remained, each about 30 centimetres high. The well shaft extended only 1 metre below the surface, and its floor was covered with gravel. East of this well stood yet another well with a frame 5.4 × 3.0 metres (fig. 10 *right*).

Around each well were ten postholes, whose distribution suggests that both wells were roofed and that the east well may have been enclosed within a small hut. Only the lowest course of panels of the frame remained around the east well. A hole pierced the frame in its southwestern corner, from which a wooden conduit led away from the well. The conduit was a 5-metre-long timber with a 30-centimetre-square cross-section. A trough, some 15 centimetres deep and in the shape of an inverted trapezoid, had been dug out of its upper surface and was completely covered with a wooden lid. As a result, only about 10 centimetres of water would stand in

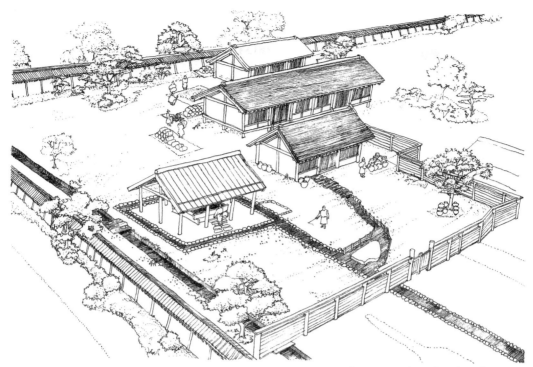

**11** Reconstruction of the area around the *Sake*-making Bureau wells. In manufacturing rice wine and rice vinegar, the *Sake*-making Bureau utilized immense quantities of water. The two large wells were to supply water for these purposes.

this well: any excess would flow down the conduit. This is a feature not normally found in wells. The conduit led to a drainage ditch; this in turn flowed into another ditch extending southward from the ditch surrounding the west well and its platform. From that juncture, the water continued to flow southward. The reconstructed situation is shown in figure 11.

This area lies in one of the shallow valleys which lead between the numerous low ridges extending like fingers southward from the hills to the north of the palace site. The valley floor is 3 to 4 metres below these ridges to its east and west, and falls away further as it continues to the south. As can be gathered from the presence of the artificial Minagami Pond at its northern end, this valley would have been a logical place to build wells. Even today, if one digs down a little into the soil near by these two wells, there will be a continuous seepage of subsurface water into the hole. In areas with such a constant supply of subsurface moisture, conditions are ideal for the preservation of artifacts. In less ideal regions, shallow subsurface preservation can be affected by surface temperature and humidity. Even at greater depths, cyclic changes in the moisture content can not only result in the loss of organic remains through decay but also affect even such objects as pottery and roof tiles. Perhaps because of the need to manufacture them in vast quantities, the Nara Palace roof tiles were fired at low temperature, with the result that many were literally half-baked. So weak were they in some cases that they seem to have returned almost to their original clay during centuries of burial. This is often true of the pottery as well. Such damage to ceramic and organic artifacts is minimized in soil where the moisture content is constant, as it is near these two wells.

Among the numerous well-preserved artifacts exhumed from the area south of the wells were over three hundred wooden tablets (*mokkan*) inscribed in China ink. They bear inscriptions such as the following (fig. 12 *left*):

> —*front surface:* Order from *Sake*-making Bureau; To Production Chiefs: Wakayue Sukunakama, Inukai Nakoto, Hiki Kusuri
> —*back surface:*  Come to work on the days specified on the Directive.

The *Sake*-making Bureau was charged with the manufacture of *sake* (the Japanese traditional brewed rice wine) and vinegar. Another tablet (fig. 12 *right*) reads:

> —*front:* Request from clerks of Auditing Bureau for 1 or 2 [a few] *gō* [180 ml.] of *sake*.
> —*back:* Supplied as requested and recorded.

The notation on the back was written in a different hand from that on the front.

Numerous other tablets make direct or indirect reference to *sake*. There are tablets which were affixed to bales of rice for *sake* making; assignment charts for the workers who hauled the water; a tablet recording the number of large storage jars.

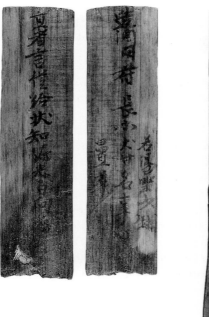

**12** Wooden tablets unearthed from the *Sake*-making Bureau remains. The discovery of wooden tablets (*mokkan*) recording the Bureau employees' work attendance (*left*) and of a *sake* requisition tablet from a different bureau (*right*) confirmed that this had been the site of the *Sake*-making Bureau.

Apart from tablets, excavation also turned up pots bearing written references to *sake*-making and the corresponding bureau. It is thus not surprising that the two large wells should have been situated here, since water, along with rice, is an indispensable ingredient in *sake*. A reasonable supposition is that the *Sake*-making Bureau itself, or one of its breweries, stood on the site. The large pots whose sherds are abundant nearby were presumably used as containers for water or *sake*.

West of the wells, in the area which had been assumed to be the site of the Great Wall's eastern section and that section's northern gate, no evidence of such structures could be found through excavation. According to old diagrams, at Heian Palace the *Sake*-making Bureau and the *Sake* Brewery (Sakadono) were located *within* the palace walls. Is it not likely that the same was true of Nara Palace? If so, where were East 1st Column Avenue and the palace's eastern border?

Another, slightly different interpretation is possible. Perhaps the palace grounds were originally square, with the wall and gate positioned as anticipated by researchers. Later in the century, the palace was expanded eastward and the *sake*-making facilities were built, at which time the wall was completely razed. When might this expansion have occurred? The bulk of the pottery in the area seems to originate in the early Nara period; at least on the grounds of morphology and technique of manufacture, it appears to predate a ceramic style which has been dated confidently to the 760s. In addition, several of the excavated wooden tablets have Japanese era dates written on them. In Western terms, the earliest date is 724 and the latest is 770.* If there was indeed an eastward expansion of the palace, the logical conclusion involving the construction of wells and other facilities is that it occurred quite soon after the original construction of the palace in 710, and the facilities would thus have been in use throughout almost the entire period of occupation of the palace.

Photographs were taken, scale drawings made, and finally the excavated earth was returned to its source. On 15 May 1965, after five and a half months, Excavation No. 22 North came to an end.

Simultaneously with this excavation, work was proceeding some 250 metres south on Excavation No. 22 South. The investigation was to cover an area of 43 ares. It was expected that an excavation of that size at that location would lay bare the remains of the Great Wall's middle east gate, a stretch of the wall to the north and south of the gate, a portion of East 1st Column Avenue running north to south just outside the wall, and the T-junction where 1st Row South Avenue flowed into East 1st Column Avenue from the east (fig. 2 gives street locations). Excavation, however, revealed no sign of the middle east gate or the wall. Instead, there was only a row of postholes for embedded pillars and several ditches. These postholes suggest the presence of nothing more than a simple board fence or

---

*Era dates have been in use since the mid-seventh century. (Previously, years were counted according to a 60-year cycle.) The government would declare a new era on the occasion of an imperial ascension, or at other times when the need was felt for spiritual renewal or for special celebration. In the eighth century alone, fifteen different eras were proclaimed, each resulting in a re-starting of the counting of years. The two dates given above correspond to the first year of Shinki and the first year of Hōki. Since 1868 eras have been re-named only on the occasion of an imperial succession; for example, the year 1989 corresponds to the 64th year of Shōwa (until 7 January) and the first year of Heisei (from 8 January).

palisade. If East 1st Column Avenue had been where it was thought to be, the ditches and fence would have blockaded it completely. Moreover, several pillared buildings also lay across the expected road site. Had the middle east gate stood where predicted, access from the outside would have been hindered by a well with a 2-metre-square frame and by a network of pebble-lined ditches (fig. 13).

As with Excavation No. 22 North, there was no sign of the expected gate nor any direct evidence of the expected avenue. On the other hand, if one was of a mind to, it was not impossible to propose that among the network of ditches there were two which had once bordered East 1st Column Avenue. The distance of 23 metres between them also seemed a reasonable width for such an avenue. Nevertheless, even if the road had indeed once lain here, from the existence of overlapping remains of buildings, wells, and the like in the vicinity of the road's surface, we may assume that the palace was rebuilt at least three times. Therefore, even if this area formerly functioned as a thoroughfare, we may be certain that the road was soon transformed into a living space containing buildings and wells, which continued to be used for a relatively long period of time.

The length of time during which the site as a whole was in use can be gathered from dates on some of the more than five hundred wooden tablets recovered. The earliest is dated 709, and others span the years from the Tempyō era (729–49) through the Jingo Keiun era (767–70). Names of various palace buildings are found on the tablets: the Sewing Bureau, the Palace Hall, and Confessionals. In terms of the people and objects mentioned, this assemblage of tablets does not differ significantly from others found *inside* the palace grounds.

**13** The wells and pillar holes excavated at the hypothesized location of East 1st Column Avenue. The abundance of features recovered from this location—supposedly outside the palace compound—confirmed that Nara Palace extended further east than the accepted theory allowed.

Other objects unearthed in the No. 22 South area also closely resemble those found within the palace. The researchers' attention was drawn in particular to the sherds of beautiful green-glazed bricks (cf. pl. 9), concentrated especially in the southeast corner of the site. In the eighth century, glazing occurred on pottery, on roof tiles, and on these bricks, which were used primarily for decorating interior walls and floors. The basic glaze consisted mainly of lead and feldspar and came out white or transparent; adding copper produced a green glaze, while adding iron yielded a yellow or brown colour. Two or three of these glazes could be used on one object. Glazed items formed a minuscule proportion of the total ceramic output: in Nara Palace, less than one piece in ten thousand was found to be glazed. It can therefore be assumed that glazed pieces were highly valued. Oddly, these green-glazed bricks had not previously been found in Nara Palace. The general opinion was that their presence here indicated that a particularly splendid building, probably the most impressive in the palace grounds, had stood on or near the spot.

At Nabunken it is the practice that a summary of the results of each year's investigations is published in the following year's *Annual Bulletin of the Nara National Cultural Properties Research Institute;* a full report is issued a few years later. The investigations on the eastern edge of the palace, conducted during 1964 and early 1965, were reported in the 1965 *Bulletin.* The following paragraph concludes the article, "A Brief Report on the Excavations and Explorations in the Nara Palace for the Year 1964":

> This year's investigations concentrated on determining the boundaries of the palace grounds. The southern and western borders were found to have remained relatively stable. On the eastern edge, however, it seems that the boundary was moved on occasion and that several buildings related to the palace were actually constructed outside the palace grounds. It remains for the future to interpret this unexpected situation. At the same time, it is necessary to consider the preservation of these features outside the palace.

Today, some twenty-five years later, one may wonder why we, the investigators, did not simply point out that the data from the excavation conflicted with previous suppositions concerning the location of East 1st Column Avenue and the eastern palace boundary, and conclude that the palace grounds extended further east than expected. Perhaps we were still under the powerful spell of the eight-*chō*-square theory to the extent that it never occurred to us that the palace grounds could have assumed another shape. The gathering of archaeological data through excavation may seem to be a highly objective process; but in the interpretation of such data, it is often difficult to break free of the spell of accepted theories. Even more so in the present case, when not only scholarly issues but also the 'practical' matter of the construction of the Nara Bypass were at stake. The results of the year's excavations were not persuasive enough to help form a new hypothesis that could both refute the conventional theory and make the bypass construction plan unfeasible. The closing paragraph of the report would perhaps serve as a warning light to the bypass construction, but further investigations would be necessary before a serious challenge could be offered to a construction plan based on the eight-*chō*-square theory.

## The fall of the eight-*chō*-square theory

Two more years and three further excavations, covering a total of 140 ares, were required to break the spell of the eight-*chō*-square theory. Excavation No. 32 lasted from December 1965 to December 1966, No. 29 from July 1966 to May 1967, and No. 39 from December 1966 to May 1967. These excavations revealed that only the southernmost quarter of the eastern palace perimeter lay where expected, with East 1st Column Avenue running just outside the Great Wall. However, at the point where East 1st Column Avenue should have formed a T-junction with 2nd Row Middle Avenue, it unexpectedly came to an end, forming instead an L-shaped junction. At the meeting point of these two roads, it had been predicted that the southernmost gate of the east wall would open to the east; instead, a gate was found blocking East 1st Column Avenue, opening to the south (fig. 14 *bottom*). To the inside of the gate stood Nara Palace.

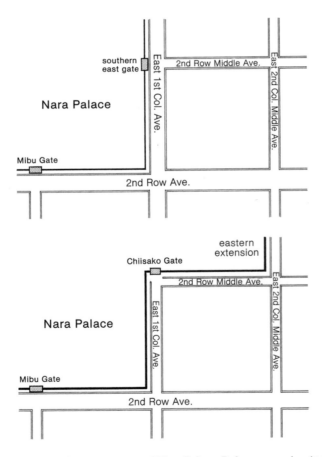

**14** The vicinity of the southeastern corner of Nara Palace. Before excavation (*top*), East 1st Column Avenue was supposed to have run directly north along the eastern edge of the palace; as a result of excavation (*bottom*), the Avenue was seen to run north only 270 m before terminating at a palace gate.

The discovery of this gate with its southward orientation provided the *coup de grâce* to the eight-*chō*-square theory. From this southern east gate,* there were ditches which ran south from the palace grounds. These ditches ran along the east and west borders of East 1st Column Avenue. They had been modified on several occasions. Both ditches held numerous artifacts, including wooden tablets. Judging from these objects, it appears that this gate was built at the time of the original construction of the palace. In other words, from the very beginning the upper three-fourths of the eastern boundary was situated further east than allowed for by the eight-*chō*-square theory.

It was now clear that the proposed Nara Bypass would cut through the Nara Palace grounds, and there was widespread demand for a change in the bypass plans. Parliamentary discussions ensued, but they did not result in a change of plans:

*9 November 1967, House of Councillors, Committee on Education:*

MEMBER SUZUKI RIKI: . . . from the standpoint of the preservation of Nara Capital, we feel that the bypass plan must be changed. . . . I'd like to inquire about the state of the government's deliberations on the matter.

FUKUHARA MASAHIKO, CHIEF SECRETARY, COMMITTEE FOR THE PROTECTION OF CULTURAL PROPERTIES (CPCP): If the palace site extends to the east, then we must respect the integrity of the site. As it stands, the bypass would run right through the site. The CPCP did agree to the Ministry of Construction's plan; however, the situation has changed since then . . . , and we have only recently arrived at the conclusion that this must be prevented at all costs. . . . I would like to meet personally with the Minister of Construction and explain the situation thoroughly. . . . The CPCP definitely wants to have the plans changed.

*21 December 1967, House of Representatives, Committee on Education, Sub-committee concerned with protection of cultural properties:*

REPRESENTATIVE MITSUBAYASHI YATARŌ: I would like to ask about the state of your negotiations with the Ministry of Construction . . . concerning the re-routing of the Route 24 bypass in order to preserve the Nara Palace site.

INADA SEISUKE, CHAIRMAN, CPCP: . . . Concerning the location of Route 24 . . . , we had visits from the Nara prefectural governor, the mayor of Nara City, and many other local people, and we were strongly urged to proceed with the plan as originally approved—the reconstruction of East 1st Column Avenue—because any change in the planned route would mean that the bypass couldn't be completed in time for the opening of Expo '70 [in Osaka]. . . . As for us . . . , any damage to the Nara Palace site would cause "five hundred, a thousand years of regrets," so we have requested that a change of route definitely be considered.

---

*In designating locations of gates, we shall adopt the convention that the second direction mentioned indicates the wall and the first (which will always have the suffix *-ern*) indicates the position of the gate in that wall. Therefore the 'southern east gate' is the southernmost gate of the eastern wall.

**15** The excavation at the East Precinct of Nara Palace. The East Precinct and its garden stood in the southern half of the eastern projection of Nara Palace.

At the time of this debate, excavations had made it clear that Nara Palace had extended much farther east than formerly believed, but it was not yet known how much farther, or exactly where the eastern boundary lay. Even if the Nara Bypass were to be moved, *how far* would it need to be moved? Further excavations would be required in order to locate the eastern edge. But where to dig?

East of the palace lay Hokkeji temple. In 738 Kōmyō, wife of Emperor Shōmu, founded Hokkeji by converting her father Fujiwara Fuhito's mansion. To build a Buddhist temple inside the palace grounds would have been unthinkable. Therefore, Fuhito's mansion must surely have stood outside the palace grounds. The road just west of Hokkeji, running north to south, should have been East 2nd Column Middle Avenue. Previous investigations had named 2nd Row Middle Avenue as the southern limit of the eastward palace extension. Proceeding from these facts, it seemed highly probable that excavation at the intersection of these two roads would reveal the southeast corner of the eastward extension.

Thus the location and purpose of Excavation No. 44 were determined. Lasting from late November 1967 until May 1968, it confirmed the expectation that the Great Wall of the palace, running from the west, would turn north at that point. The eastern border of the palace was indeed East 2nd Column Middle Avenue. Nara Palace extended nearly 270 metres further east than originally thought. In 'eight-*chō*-square' terms, the extension measured 6 *chō* north to south and 2 *chō* east to west, and the palace grounds as a whole were 10 *chō* east to west.

At the same time, the section of the grounds just inside the southeastern corner was excavated. Among the features revealed were an irregular-shaped pond demarcated by fist-sized natural rocks, with a small island and decorative garden rock for-

**16** Reconstruction of the East Precinct garden at Nara Palace.

mations; a curving ditch paved with rocks 20 to 30 centimetres in size; a pillared building which extended partly over the pond; and, just inside the corner of the wall, a singular octagonal structure facing the pond (figs. 15, 16). The pillars of this octagonal building were set much more firmly than usual, suggesting that it was more than one storey high.

This pond-and-garden area yielded many green-glazed bricks identical to those found during Excavation No. 22 South, Excavation No. 39 which revealed the Great Wall's southern east gate, and Excavation No. 43 which was later carried out in the region between No. 22 South and No. 39. Some green-glazed and three-coloured roof tiles were also recovered (pl. 9). As elsewhere, most roof tiles at Nara Palace were unglazed—in fact, these are the only glazed ones to be found there. A passage for the year 767 in the *Shoku Nihongi* chronicle of the period comes to mind: 'The Jewelled Hall of the East Precinct was completed. This building was roofed with lapis-lazuli roof tiles, so people called it the Jewelled Palace.' Presumably we can equate the 'lapis-lazuli roof tiles' with the green-glazed and three-coloured roof tiles mentioned above. The monarch at this time, Empress Shōtoku (reigned 764–70), sometimes held ceremonies and banquets in the East Precinct. It would hardly be surprising that it did indeed have such a garden. Thus we are presumably safe in concluding that Nara Palace's eastward extension—at least its southern portion—contained the East Precinct. A banquet was held in the East Precinct in the first month of the sixth year of Tempyō Shōhō era (754).* The

*It must be remembered that the traditional East Asian 12-lunar-month calendar lags variably behind the Gregorian by an average of about a month; thus, the first day of the first month falls somewhere between about 15 January and 15 February.

*Man'yōshū (Collection of Ten Thousand Leaves)*, a poetry anthology compiled in the eighth century, contains a poem read on that occasion and refers to the banquet's location as the East Palace. The East Palace was the residence of the crown prince. The East Palace of Nara Palace can be traced back to 714 in written records, and was presumably occupied by successive crown princes. Later it was also called the Mountain Plum Palace.

Thus the facilities in the southeastern corner of the eastern extension seem to have changed name from East Palace to East Precinct to Mountain Plum Palace as well as undergoing some physical alterations. In any case, their importance continued throughout the eighth century. The garden pond, which was only partially exposed during Excavation No. 44, was completely uncovered during subsequent investigations. This pond was found to have undergone extensive alteration during the mid-eighth century and to have continued to exist until at least the early ninth century. Judging by a name inscribed on a wooden tablet found nearby, this garden may also have been called the East Garden.

The determination of the eastern boundary and of the presence of important buildings in the area led inevitably to the necessity for reformulating the bypass plans. A nation-wide preservation movement sprang up in 1966, led by the Council to Oppose Routing the Nara Bypass through the Nara Palace Site. This movement combined with parliamentary pressure to accelerate the pace of deliberations between the CPCP and the Ministry of Construction.

*9 March 1968, House of Representatives, Committee on Budget:*

REPRESENTATIVE HASEGAWA SHŌZŌ: I think we must rapidly change the Route 24 bypass plans and guarantee the preservation of the Nara Palace site. . . .

HORI SHIGERU, CONSTRUCTION MINISTER: . . . We don't intend to force anything through. . . . A historic site isn't something that can be replaced, so I have given an order that there must be sufficient consultation with the CPCP, and that there will be no construction without everyone's consent.

*4 April 1968, House of Councillors, Committee on Construction:*

MEMBER ŌMORI HISASHI: . . . Because of plans to build a bypass, the Nara Palace site was excavated with funding from the Ministry of Construction and from local sources. The investigations unexpectedly turned up the East Precinct. This suggests that both the Ministry of Education and the scholars involved have until now been very sloppy in their investigations. The palace, a site of great importance, had of course been investigated extensively even before the construction question arose. It had been researched for two years. Then, when the bypass issue was taken up . . . , for the first time we learn that they have found the East Precinct. Such unreliable investigation and research causes great trouble to us local residents. . . . I'd like to ask whether you will be able, sincerely and responsibly, to revise the route and complete construction in time for Expo '70 in Osaka.

CONSTRUCTION MINISTER HORI: . . . The significance of the Route 24 bypass, with the opening of Expo '70 as a target, is very great. . . . The government is determined to finish in time somehow, removing all hindrance, so we must earnestly request the fullest local co-operation.

*24 April 1968, House of Representatives, Committee on Education:*

REPRESENTATIVE HASEGAWA SHŌZŌ: . . . Concerning the preservation of Nara Palace . . . , I'd like to ask for a report on the course of events.

FUKUHARA MASAHIKO, CHIEF SECRETARY, CPCP: . . . It has been decided that the bypass will not pass through the Nara Palace site. At present, the Construction Bureau is considering alternative routes. (Applause.) I would like to express my sincerest gratitude.

The new route, decided in September 1968, approached the northeast corner of the palace from the north and ran parallel to the National Railway's Kansai Line. As it entered the territory of the ancient capital, it headed south along the former East 3rd Column Avenue, bending sharply to the west as it crossed the former 2nd Row Middle Avenue. Near the southeastern corner of the palace grounds it once again bent south and continued, as originally planned, down East 1st Column Avenue (see fig. 8). The bypass, avoiding the Nara Palace site, was opened in the autumn of 1971—one year after the end of Expo '70.

Since the seventeenth century, or perhaps even earlier, Nara Palace had been believed to measure eight *chō* square. Modern research since the late nineteenth century continued to support this theory. Then in a span of four years, through excavation of a mere 3 hectares, the bottom dropped out of this theory. In reality, what had been accepted as historical fact was no more than a hypothesis based on written sources, contemporary topography, and comparison with other ancient capitals. The hypothesis could only be evaluated through excavation. Confronted with the harsh reality of the threat to the Nara Palace site and the changes in the bypass plans, we researchers were forced once again to mull over this elementary fact: archaeology, indeed, all sciences, had to live with hypotheses.

# Chapter 2

# Excavation, Hypotheses, and Evidence

### The collapse of a theory: The gates of the Great Wall

Conventional opinions are like dominos: topple one, and others may begin to fall. The demise of the eight-*chō*-square theory had a ripple effect on several other assumptions about Nara Palace. One of these concerned the gates of the Great Wall. It had been assumed that there were a total of twelve gates in the palace's outer wall, three on each of the four sides. The basis for this assumption was an annotation from the year 738 added to the Taihō Codes, a body of law promulgated in 701: 'In the outermost four walls there are twelve large gates.' For information concerning the names and positions of these gates, however, it had been necessary to depend entirely on comparisons with Nagaoka Palace and Heian Palace. The results of this hypothesis are shown in figure 17.

The outer gates at Heian Palace were given fashionable and elegant two-character Chinese-style names in 818. Prior to that, it was believed, each gate had been named after the family responsible for guarding it. These families had long been intimately involved with military affairs and were close advisers to the emperor. Most had traditionally served as palace guards under the supervision of the Ōtomo family. Thus, so the reasoning went, the palace gates were named after these families.

Names of several outer gates are recorded in the *Shoku Nihongi* chronicle. At Fujiwara Palace, the immediate precursor to Nara Palace, there was an Amainukai Gate. Nara Palace itself had Naka-no-Mibu Gate, Ikuha Gate, and, according to another eighth-century document, Takerube Gate. These names agree quite closely with those at Nagaoka and the early Heian Palace. It seemed, then, that the names of the outer palace gates were traditionally assigned and passed on with little change whenever the capital was relocated. On that basis, it was reasonable to extrapolate backward from Nagaoka and Heian Palaces in order to reconstruct the names and locations of the Nara gates.

The reconstruction, however, was based on the premise that the eight-*chō*-square pattern was applicable to Nara Palace. With square palace grounds and twelve gates, there should have been three gates on each side. But the premise collapsed. With the discovery of the eastern extension, the palace's ground plan now took the shape of a rectangle extending east to west with a section missing from its southeast corner. The northwest corner of the missing section lay at the point which the eight-*chō*-square theory predicted to be the site of the east wall's southern gate (in

32

our terminology, the 'southern east gate'). Instead, a gate was found slightly to the east of this point, facing outwards to the south and blocking East 1st Column Avenue (see fig. 14 *bottom*). Naturally, no such gate was known at Nagaoka or Heian.

Just outside this gate, several wooden tablets were recovered from the ditch along the west side of East 1st Column Avenue. On some of these, the name of a gate was recorded. The job of guarding the palace gates and controlling passage of goods and persons fell to the Office of Gate Guardians. Inspection of goods, especially military items, was most rigorous at the gates of the Great Wall, where the palace came into contact with the outer world. Such goods could enter or leave the grounds only upon presentation of the appropriate documents. The latter specified the type and quantity of goods to be passed, the designated gate of passage, the person responsible for the transit, and so forth. It is highly probable that the tablets bearing gate names served as the necessary credentials. One of these grants permission for the passage of horse feed to the officer overseeing construction of a palace building called the East Domicile. Another seems to pertain to military goods. Presumably the guard would check the tablet against the orders in his gate register before granting passage. Once outside the gate, the tablets were no longer needed and apparently were tossed into the roadside ditch. These were not the only two examples.

The gate named on these two tablets was written with Chinese characters 小子 meaning 'small child'. In Japanized Chinese, these characters would be read

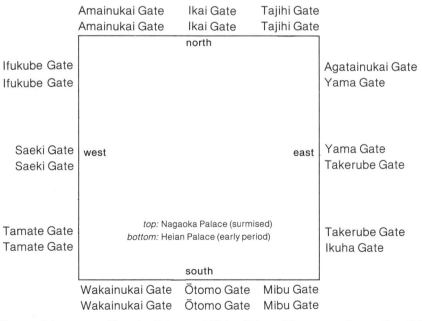

**17** Names of the gates at Nagaoka Palace and Heian Palace. The names of most Nara Palace gates had been hypothesized to be identical with those of either Nagaoka Palace or Heian Palace which have survived in the documents.

Shōshi; in 'pure' Japanese, Chiisako. (See the discussion in Chapter 1 concerning the names Nara and Heijō, pp. 5–6.) Let us assume for the present that this gate was called Chiisako Gate. It was then most likely under the guardianship of a *be* named Chiisako. *Be* is usually translated as 'clan', although in some cases it corresponds more closely to the notion of a 'localized work group'. (For details, see the entry on *be* in the *Kodansha Encyclopedia of Japan*, published by Kodansha International.) There is a theory that the Chiisako *be* was a clan made up of young persons, having a military character, and serving closely the imperial institution. In this sense, it would have been a suitable clan for the gate-guarding duties.

No gate by this name is recorded at either Nagaoka or Heian Palace, but there appears to have been a Chiisako Gate at Fujiwara Palace. The plan of Fujiwara Palace was nearly square, so it is hypothesized that there were three gates on each of the four outer walls. Excavations have so far located the middle and western gates of the south wall, the middle gate of the north wall, the northern gate of the east wall, and the southern gate of the west wall. Evidence from wooden tablets seems to confirm the existence in the north wall of Tajihi and Ikai Gates, and in the east wall of Takerube, Yamabe, and Chiisako-be Gates. (Unlike the Chiisako Gate at Nara Palace, the word *be* is included in the gate name—as indeed it is also for Takerube and Yamabe Gates.) The contribution of archaeological evidence to our knowledge becomes apparent when one considers that only a single Fujiwara gate name, Amainukai, occurs in documentary sources. At any rate, the Fujiwara evidence increases our confidence that the gate at Nara Palace was indeed the Chiisako Gate.

Are we then to assume that any gate name occurring on a tablet must be that of the nearest gate? Near the western gate of Nara Palace's south wall, another tablet has surfaced bearing the name Chiisako-be Gate. It is doubtful that there were two palace gates with the same name. Which, if either, of these two gates, then, bore that name? To further complicate the matter, a tablet bearing the name Wakainukai Gate was also found near the western south gate. The inscription on this latter tablet suggests that it was issued in the fourth month of 736 by the West Buddha Hall construction office to a person charged with buying lumber. Carrying cash, he was to proceed via Wakainukai Gate to Izumi-no-tsu, a harbour on the Kizu River some 5 kilometres north of Nara Palace. The layout of the contents of this tablet resembles those found near our presumed Chiisako Gate. Quite possibly, then, this western south gate was called Wakainukai Gate, and the presence nearby of a tablet referring to Chiisako-be Gate has some other explanation. As further support, the western south gate at Heian Palace was also called Wakainukai Gate at first. (In the subsequent wave of sinophilia it was renamed Kōka Gate.) It was also called Utamai-no-Tsukasa Gate, since the Music Bureau (Utamai-no-Tsukasa, Gagaku-ryō) was originally situated just inside the gate. Perhaps the sounds of the palace musicians at practice carried to the vicinity of the gate. Back at Nara, near the Wakainukai tablet, two potsherds were found on which were written the words 'Music Bureau' and 'music' (fig. 18). Surely these sherds belonged to vessels intended for use in the Music Bureau, and we can assume that, at Nara as at the earliest phase of Heian, this bureau stood near the western south gate. Thus various lines of evidence point to this as Wakainukai Gate.

What then of the tablet labelled Chiisako-be Gate found near Wakainukai Gate? It granted permission to a representative of the Inner Catering Bureau (which was in charge of preparing meals for the immediate imperial family) to bring salt, seaweed, and other marine products into the grounds via Chiisako-be Gate. But this tablet was found in a ditch just *inside* the western south gate. Can we not assume that the provisioner, having delivered the goods to a spot near this gate, tossed the tablet into the nearest ditch? Given that the preponderance of evidence favours this gate being Wakainukai Gate, we must also assume that he carried the tablet all the way from the southern east gate—our putative Chiisako(-be) Gate—before disposing of it.

Looking at all lines of evidence for gate names from Fujiwara Palace up to Heian Palace, there appears to have been little change in the names of the gates in the south and west walls and possibly of those in the north wall. Today scholars are inclined to think that there was considerably less continuity from Fujiwara through Nara to Nagaoka and Heian in the gate names of the eastern side, due to the special addition of the eastern projection at Nara Palace. Against this background, the majority view is that the western south gate at Nara was called Wakainukai, just as at Fujiwara and Heian, while Chiisako(-be) referred to a gate in the east wall at both Fujiwara and Nara.

This view has been strengthened by the accumulating weight of experience favouring archaeological evidence over the often unreliable documentary sources. However, as the example of the gate names demonstrates, the interpretation of archaeological sources also requires repeated reformulation and evaluation of

**18**
Sherds from a vessel inscribed with the name 'Music Bureau'. The western south gate of Nara Palace is Wakainukai Gate; however, the gate in this same position at Heian Palace was given the additional name of Music Bureau Gate. At Nara Palace also, these potsherds were found near this gate, suggesting that the Music Bureau stood nearby.

hypotheses and premises. For example, it is obviously not necessarily the case that artifacts—including wooden tablets—have been discarded in the place where they were used. We should thus be extremely cautious when creating hypotheses based on the place of excavation. Nevertheless, if we are to maintain that the western south gate at Fujiwara was named Wakainukai, then we have no choice but to assume that the Wakainukai tablet was discarded near its place of use while the Chiisako-be tablet, by contrast, was for some reason abandoned at a considerable distance from its point of use. That is to say, from the standpoint of dealing with the materials, we are by no means free from the criticism of arbitrariness. In research which deals with excavated artifacts as historiographical source materials, we are still far from establishing a methodology equal to the potential of these materials.

Excavation of six of the outer wall gates at Nara Palace has been completed: the three in the front (i.e., south) wall, the middle and southern gates of the west wall, and the southern gate of the eastern projection. The Outer Gates on the northern edge and the eastern extension now await investigation. The discovery of the eastern extension makes it difficult to know where to look for some of the remaining gates. There are other problems too. For example, at Heian, the eastern north gate was named Tajihi Gate. If we project its position onto Nara Palace without adjustment, it falls directly on top of a round hillock 10 metres tall and 100 metres across. This hillock originally formed the mound of one of the keyhole-shaped tumuli of the fifth century. The front platform of the tumulus, which would have extended into the palace grounds, was razed at the time of palace construction (fig. 19). With such an imposing mound on this spot, could there ever have been a palace gate there? If not, then where? We must await the results of future excavations.

### Reconstructing lost objects: The case of Scarlet Phoenix Gate

'Scarlet Phoenix' Gate, midway along the front wall of the palace grounds, was the principal gate for the entire compound. Not surprisingly, it was the first to be excavated. The meagre remains (fig. 20) provide a surprising amount of evidence. Let us summarize what has been learned so far. In constructing this gate, the topsoil was first scraped away over quite a broad area, exposing a substrate free of human interference. A rectangular trench was then dug, 33.5 metres east to west, 16.2 metres north to south, and 1.5 metres deep. The bottom of the trench was covered with a layer of smooth stones 20 to 30 centimetres in diameter. Over this a mixture of sandy and clayey soils was tamped firmly into place. This procedure was repeated until the trench was filled with tamped earth and then continued further until a considerable mound had been produced, to serve as the foundation or podium for the gate.

Shallow holes were dug in the podium, and a base stone to support a pillar was partially embedded in each hole. These base stones were flat on top but irregular underneath; so-called root stones, some 20–30 centimetres in size, were wedged under them for stabilization (see fig. 9 *bottom right*).

In later times, however, this podium for Scarlet Phoenix Gate was entirely levelled. The base stones and their holes have thus disappeared almost completely:

**19** A mounded tomb destroyed during Nara Palace construction. There are many fifth-century mounded tombs north of Nara Palace. Even in excavations of the palace itself, the southeastern corner of the keyhole-shaped tomb and its surrounding moat (the larger tomb of the two in the *top* photo) have been discovered, revealing that the tombs which fell within the palace precincts at the time of construction were razed.

only the bottom portion of the holes and a few of the root stones remain. The carefully dressed stone slabs that had once coated the surface and sides of the podium, the wooden superstructure of the gate itself, and the stairsteps and rain gutters that must have been a part of the podium all disappeared when the podium was razed.

The scant remains nevertheless provide some information concerning the wooden superstructure of the gate proper. The following five conclusions may be drawn.

1. The pillars stood in three rows of six each, spaced equidistantly like the intersections of lines on graph paper.
2. Measured from centre to centre as was customary, the pillars were separated by 5.05 metres, or 17 *shaku* in the units of the time.
3. Judging from the presence of root stones, each pillar must have rested on a large base stone.
4. Since numerous roof tiles have been recovered from the area near the gate, it must have had a tiled roof.
5. Judging by the dimensions of the trench remains, the podium must have extended some 12 *shaku* beyond the rows of pillars supporting the structure.

In truth, these five points are the only certainties available to us in attempting to reconstruct Scarlet Phoenix Gate.

From there on, the assumptions begin. Three eighth-century gates survive, all in

**20**  Remains of Scarlet Phoenix Gate. These are the excavated remains of Scarlet Phoenix Gate, which served as the front entrance to Nara Palace. This gate was constructed with three rows of six pillars each, as revealed in the layout of base stones.

Buddhist temples. With these as reference points (figs. 21, 22), we can marshal evidence from gates of later periods as well as from other extant examples of eighth-century architecture, yielding the following image of Scarlet Phoenix Gate. Seen from the front, its pillars stood in six columns, each three rows deep. The six pillars of the nearest and farthest rows would have stood unconnected by wall panels, exposed to the elements, while the pillars of the middle row were linked by sections of wall or by doors. Comparative documentary and pictorial evidence suggests that the outer two bays (spaces between pillars) of the middle row would have contained walls while the inner three held the doors.

Next, what of the gate's basic design? Was it one storey high or two? Was the roof gabled, hipped, or hip-gabled? Absolutely no clues survive in the archaeological record. On these points too, we have no choice but to rely on the comparative evidence provided by architectural historians. The main gate of a palace such as Nara should have been an imposing structure of the highest calibre— presumably, therefore, a two-storey gate with a hip-gable roof. This was the case with Scarlet Phoenix Gate at Heian Palace, as depicted in a scroll which comes down to us from the end of the twelfth century. Consider also the podium, so exactingly constructed with its several subterranean layers of packed earth. Surely it was intended to support a structure of impressive dimensions with more than one storey.

The base stones are gone. No trace of the pillars remains. Judging by other ancient gates and buildings, the pillars might have been approximately 2.5 *shaku* in diameter. We may suppose that their height was equal to the distance between them, 17 *shaku*. They would have had the slightly convex silhouette, the gently swollen waistline called entasis, characteristic of pillars in ancient Greece as well as at Japan's renowned seventh-century Hōryūji temple (fig. 22). But what sort of capital crowned each pillar? If a two-storey gate, then what was the height of each storey? There would have been a railing around the perimeter of the upper storey, but of what design? What about the slope of the roof? How far did the eaves overhang the pillars? Seen from the front, the line of the eaves was probably not straight but curved upwards at either end. How sharply did they curve? How were the roof tiles laid? Of what style were the doors? What of the metal fittings? Using all available information from architectural history and from archaeology, together with a healthy dose of common sense and occasional aesthetic judgement, the attempt to reconstruct the gate continues (see fig. 23).

At a meeting to discuss possibilities for the gate's reconstruction, a certain phrase came up which gives an impression of the nature of the interaction between scholarship and pragmatism: '*osamari ga yoi*'. Each specialist carries various images based on extensive experience in the back of his or her mind. These images reflect matters ranging from the tiniest details of ancient architecture to the broadest overviews. When a particular reconstruction plan matches those images, one says that *osamari ga yoi*, that is, the plan is 'well-arranged'. A well-arranged plan can only emerge as a result of various choices based on these images. Naturally, researchers may prefer different plans depending on their own images. When more than one researcher is involved in the formulation of a plan, the result will usually be the common denominator emerging from the individual images. This phenomenon is not

**23** Reconstruction of Scarlet Phoenix Gate. Scarlet Phoenix Gate can be hypothetically reconstructed as this kind of structure, with reference to extant eighth-century buildings.

*opposite page*

**21** *(top)* Tegai Gate, Tōdaiji temple. There are three extant gates dating to the eighth century, the Tegai Gate being one of them. It is the northernmost of the gates opening to the west at Tōdaiji temple.

**22** *(bottom)* Middle Gate, Hōryūji temple. This gate, in the Western Precinct of Hōryūji temple, is the world's oldest extant wooden structure. Completed in the early eighth century, it is noted for the entasis, or gently bulging profile, of its pillars.

limited to the reconstruction of buildings. The same process ensues when the object is to reconstruct a concrete image of a past society, its culture, and its way of life, whether through written sources or through excavation.

Apart from Scarlet Phoenix Gate, five other gates of the Great Wall have been excavated and examined in detail. On the east side is Chiisako Gate. On the west side, there is the middle gate (called Saeki Gate at Heian Palace) and the southern gate (named Tamate Gate). The western and eastern south gates have also been examined. The former is our Wakainukai Gate, while the latter is called Naka-no-Mibu Gate in the *Shoku Nihongi* chronicle. How does the evidence from these five gates compare with our conclusions about Scarlet Phoenix Gate?

The packed-earth trenches of the two gates of the west wall are slightly smaller than those of Scarlet Phoenix Gate, about 30 by 14 metres. The workmanship in these trenches is also inferior to that at Scarlet Phoenix Gate. No base stones survive, but the pillars appear to have stood in a six-by-three matrix as at Scarlet Phoenix Gate. However, although the spacing of the pillars along the longer north-south dimension was apparently 17 *shaku* as at Scarlet Phoenix Gate, the shorter east-west spacing may have been slightly smaller at about 15 *shaku*. Considering the less careful construction of the trenches, these lesser gates on the side wall may have been only one storey high. Perhaps they also had simpler, gabled roofs rather than hip-gable (fig. 24). Still, these are only hypotheses.

As for the front wall, the trench of the eastern gate is almost the same size as those of the two other gates, but no evidence concerning the positions of the pillars

**24** Reconstruction of the middle west gate of the Great Wall. Although Scarlet Phoenix Gate was probably a monumental two-storeyed construction, the other gates were likely to have been more modest structures such as this.

survives. The western gate (Wakainukai) has a pillar placement identical to that of Scarlet Phoenix. Chiisako Gate, in the east wall, seems to have been smaller than the other gates. While the existing conditions of the structural remains are very poor, thus precluding any detailed investigation, we may conclude that the Chiisako Gate podium was at least 5 metres narrower in width than the other outer gates, even if we assume that the gate completely blocked off East 1st Column Avenue from the south (see fig. 14 *bottom*).

## Excavation and hypothesis formulation

Under the surface of present-day Nara lie the remains of Nara Palace; we have only to excavate in order to find the clues necessary for reconstructing its ancient form. Today, this is well known. In the mid-nineteenth century, however, Kitaura Sadamasa did not know this; nor did Sekino Tadashi when he published his research results at the start of the present century. Then, around 1910, a movement to recognize the importance of Nara Palace began. As one element in the programme, a part of the palace site was purchased with donations and later given to the state authorities, who began work on the preservation of the site. This was around 1924–25. During the ensuing ground work, features such as base stones and corridor podia came to light. These discoveries were described in a research report published in 1925, the first publication pertaining to subterranean features at Nara Palace. In 1928 and 1932 prefectural engineer Kishi Kumakichi conducted the first excavations on the site in the northeastern sector of what would have been the palace grounds according to the eight-*chō*-square theory. His excavations revealed a large ditch, 2 metres across and 1.5 metres deep, its banks reinforced with river stones and containing numerous artifacts.

Excavations at the palace began in earnest, however, only after the Second World War. As mentioned earlier, the first of these was in 1953 in conjunction with the widening of the road commonly called 1st Row Road (Ichijō-dōri), which cut east-to-west through the northern part of the palace site. The road, originally barely able to accommodate an oxcart, was widened to a full two lanes. The national government had already designated the Nara Palace site as a Historic Site in 1922 and upgraded it to Special Historic Site in 1952. Sites with these designations could not be tampered with or altered without permission. The CPCP, the body then in charge of policy dealing with cultural properties, granted permission for the road-works on the condition that the existing road would simply be widened, without eliminating the old road surface. At the same time, the Main Hall of Hokkeji temple, an Important Cultural Property to the east of the palace site, was undergoing renovation and rebuilding under the direction of prefectural engineer Okada Sōji. On his way to and from work Okada had to walk between Hokkeji and Saidaiji Station, which took him past the road-works at the Nara Palace site. One day his eye was caught by areas of different-coloured earth in a ditch which had been dug alongside the road. Might these not indicate the holes for embedded pillars? As the changes in colour were at regular intervals and extended quite a distance, Okada was certain they must be the postholes of a building.

His discovery was the first to confirm that a so-called 'embedded-pillar building' existed at Nara Palace—or anywhere within Nara Capital, for that matter. In such structures, the pillars were set, that is, embedded, directly into a hole dug in the ground; the hole was then re-filled around the pillar (see fig. 9 *bottom left*). Sometimes, but not often, a stone or board would be laid in the hole beneath the pillar. In contrast to these embedded-pillar buildings were what we call 'base-stone buildings'. Their pillars, rather than standing in deep postholes, rest on base stones laid on the surface or occasionally, as in the case of Scarlet Phoenix Gate, laid in a shallow hole (see fig. 9 *bottom right*). All extant eighth-century buildings are base-stone buildings; no embedded-pillar buildings survive from that century. When a base-stone building is razed and the earth levelled, nearly all trace is lost. Little information is available through excavation in such cases. In the case of the outer palace gates, of the six so far excavated, pillar placements could be determined for only two, and even the size of the podium was unclear in some cases. Had it not been for the subsurface, packed-earth portion of the podia, that is, had the base stones simply been placed on unprepared ground as usual, we might not have even realized that a building had stood on the spot.

Embedded-pillar buildings are much more likely to occur as archaeological features than are base-stone buildings. The postholes vary in size and shape. At Nara most are about 1 metre square and 1 metre deep. But there are some gigantic postholes; one, for example, is a rectangle, 3.5 by 2.5 metres and 2.8 metres deep. Even if the original surface of the period has been slightly shaved away, the lower part of the posthole at least will usually survive, allowing us to determine the presence of a building and its approximate scale. Moreover, even granting that the rate of survival of base-stone buildings is low in general, it does seem that embedded-pillar buildings were particularly numerous at Nara. For this reason, excavation should easily yield results.

The embedded pillars themselves tended to be circular, about 1 *shaku* in diameter. The diameter was usually 10 to 12 per cent of the distance between the pillars: a separation of 3 metres suggests a diameter of about 30 centimetres. However, for taller, multi-storey buildings, the pillars naturally had to be thicker to support the additional weight. For example, in the case of the gigantic postholes mentioned above, although the spacing between pillars was only 4.5 metres, each pillar was some 75 centimetres in diameter—and the location was indeed suitable for a multi-storey pagoda-like pavilion. It is not uncommon for a part of the base of an embedded pillar to survive (fig. 25). From these survivals, we know that the most common material for the pillars was Japanese cypress (*hinoki; Chamaecyparis obtusa* [Sieb. et Zucc.] Endl.), followed by Japanese umbrella pine (*kōyamaki; Sciadopitys verticillata* [Thunb.] Sieb. et Zucc.).

The first archaeologist to identify an embedded-pillar building at a site was the German Carl Schuchhardt. It was during excavations begun in 1899 at Haltern, the site of a Roman fort in what is now the state of Nordrhein-Westfalen. The importance of embedded-pillar postholes for determining past structures was summed up by Schuchhardt in the words: 'Nichts ist eben dauerhafter als ein ordentliches Loch'—'Nothing is as durable as a proper hole.' The first Japanese to find an embedded-pillar hole was the architectural historian Asano Kiyoshi, during an investigation in 1934 at the world's oldest surviving wooden building, Hōryūji temple. Asano, to whom the field of architectural history is indebted for several impressive advances in methodology, also made a considerable contribution to archaeology. His major contribution was to conduct excavations in search of the subsurface remains of ancient buildings, in the process of which an important clue was confirming the existence of embedded-pillar holes.

That Okada Sōji, director of repairs at Hokkeji temple, should have to walk by the road-works at the Nara Palace site each day in November 1953 was an unimaginable stroke of luck. Hokkeji was converted into a Buddhist convent by the imperial consort Kōmyō in the middle of the eighth century, having previously been the mansion of her father, Fujiwara Fuhito. Although Okada was officially in charge of the renovation work at Hokkeji, it was Asano Kiyoshi who directed all details of the disassembling, repair, and reassembling of the Main Hall. During the archaeological excavation accompanying this work, embedded-pillar building remains, which were assumed to have been part of Fuhito's mansion, had come to light. Thus Okada had already had practical experience of embedded-pillar holes. News of Okada's discovery at Nara Palace was brought to the Cultural Properties Preservation Section of the Nara Prefectural Board of Education. Immediately the order was given to halt construction and to begin excavation. Thus it was that the Board of Education began its excavation on 2 December 1953, and the CPCP conducted its own investigation from 12 to 29 January of the following year. The investigating team was an *ad hoc* body involving specialists drawn from several institutions, including Nabunken, Nara National Museum, Nara Women's

**25**
Embedded-pillar bases. For buildings constructed with pillars embedded in the ground, the bases often survive within the postholes.

University, Nara University of Arts and Science (today's Nara University of Education), and the prefectural Board of Education.

The results of the excavations ushered in a new era in the history of investigations at Nara Palace, and not only because of the confirmation of the existence of embedded-pillar buildings. From postholes and base stones it was determined that there had once been a mammoth building on the site, as much as 100 metres long. Furthermore—and this is of particular importance to us—it was found that traces of three structures overlapped in a single location: two embedded-pillar buildings and one base-stone building. Clearly these had been built at three different times. The discovery of this important fact was due directly to the participation of Asano and other architectural historians as the principal actors in the examination and identification of features. The archaeologists who participated at that time cannot be credited with much active involvement in the examination of *features*, for they seemed to view their primary task as the collection of *artifacts* such as roof tiles and pottery. It was not until Nara Palace Excavation No. 1 of 1955 that archaeologists began to contribute actively to excavation and to collaborate with the architectural historians in survey and research.

The architectural historians excavated features in order to prove their hypotheses about the actual forms of ancient buildings. If the features of a certain location lead to the assumption of two separate buildings, it follows that they could not have existed simultaneously and must therefore have been built at different times. But how to prove which had come first? The methods for making such a determination, which are now considered common knowledge among archaeologists, were at that time still the exclusive property of the more advanced architectural historians.

The overlapping of features, and the resulting hypothesis that construction had taken place within the Nara Palace grounds at several different times, brought a new perspective to research on the palace site. When Kitaura Sadamasa undertook the task of ascertaining the street plan of Nara Capital and the position and extent of the palace, he was satisfied with merely noting the presence of several place-names evocative of palace buildings and then recording these on his reconstructed map of Nara Capital. Sekino Tadashi compared references to palace buildings from written sources with the local topography and traces of palace earthworks remaining between agricultural fields, in order to establish hypotheses about the location of various palace buildings (see fig. 26).

It presumably never seriously occurred to Sekino that the position of some of the buildings might have changed considerably during the period of Nara Palace's existence. Most subsequent analysts, under the strong influence of Sekino's research, also adopted this, shall we say 'static', viewpoint. Beginning with Asano, however, many architectural historians became acquainted with actual cases where, for example, a palace hall had been replaced first by a Buddhist temple building with embedded pillars and later by a base-stone building—all on the same spot. Not only the buildings but their functions had changed. Furthermore, from his own experience with the repair and rebuilding of ancient structures, Asano was able to develop the methodology for determining the changes that had taken place in a single building from its original form through successive renovations. It was an attitude that saw buildings, their earthworks, and overall sites as continually changing. With the results of the excavations of 1953 and 1954, a similar attitude was adopted by the excavators, who now felt that Nara Palace had to be seen not in a static but in a dynamic context. This new attitude would give birth to new interpretations of Nara Palace.

In August 1955, in unusually hot and humid weather, the Nara Basin filled with researchers from Nabunken, the Tokyo National Museum, Nara Women's University, Nara Prefectural Board of Education, and other interested organizations, who had come to carry out further excavations at the Nara Palace site. They had gathered for the second excavation since the end of the war and the first excavation ever organized for a purely academic motive, that is, to determine the actual condition of the palace site. For the excavation, they selected an area in the eastern part of the palace grounds, about 70 metres southeast of a large-scale earthen platform thought to have been the podium for the Great Supreme Hall. This spot fell within what Sekino had surmised to be the State Halls Compound.

Based on a review of the research done on Heian Palace from the tenth century onwards and the references to Nara Palace in eighth-century manuscripts, it was thought that Nara Palace had been an agglomeration of several discrete nuclear palace districts. One of these was the Imperial Domicile, the living quarters of the emperor and the royal family. Another was the Great Supreme Hall Compound, centred on the Great Supreme Hall, where the emperor conducted the affairs and ceremonies of state. Directly in front (to the south) of this precinct was the State Halls Compound, consisting of twelve symmetrically disposed buildings. This compound was also referred to as the Twelve Halls. Here ceremonies of imperial succession took place as did many sorts of rites and banquets. Directly in front of this compound were the Morning Assembly Halls, a pair of buildings symmetrically placed to the right and left (see fig. 27).

High-ranking court officials were expected to appear each morning at the State Halls Compound—the so-called Morning Visit. Originally *all* officials were to attend, but as the number of officials grew along with the bureaucracy, only the upper ranks were required to appear. First they would enter the Morning Assembly Halls and change into Morning Dress; then at the appointed time they moved to designated seats in the Twelve Halls. Apparently the higher-ranking officials would then walk to the plaza in front of the Great Supreme Hall to offer Morning Obeisance to the emperor before beginning their Morning Duties. These duties completed, the officials would repair to their own offices, which also stood within the palace grounds, and attend to the business of the day. These buildings were then the principal components of the palace, but there were also other buildings, gardens, ponds, and so forth, such as the East Precinct.

Sekino Tadashi knew from literary sources of the existence of the South Garden, a site for banquets and ceremonies. In his view (fig. 26), it stood just inside Scarlet Phoenix Gate, occupying the central portion of the grounds. He envisaged the Imperial Domicile as standing directly north of the garden. To the garden's east, occupying one-third of the grounds, Sekino placed the Great Supreme Hall and the State Halls Compound with the East Precinct to their north. He placed the West

Palace, which was known from written sources, near the western edge of the grounds. In the area where he envisaged the Great Supreme Hall and State Halls Compound there was a very wide earthen platform. The local residents called this platform Daikoku-no-shiba or Daikokuden (virtually homonymous with Daigoku-den, or Great Supreme Hall), and it was widely assumed to be the remains of the podium of the ancient hall. In the fields to the south of this platform could be seen various smaller platforms, set in pairs. This pattern brought to mind the State Halls Compound and the Morning Assembly Halls. Given these conditions, Sekino's suppositions were widely viewed as highly probable, indeed as almost certainly accurate.

This area, which Sekino had concluded was the Great Supreme Hall/State Halls Compound precinct, was donated to the state during the 1920s, as a result of the movement to honour and preserve Nara Palace. The Nara Palace site, including this package of land, was declared a Historic Site in 1922 under the terms of the Law for the Preservation of Historic Sites, Places of Scenic Beauty and Natural Monuments. During 1924–25, protective measures were taken and a moat was dug around the land which had been donated to the state. Ueda Sampei, who had been commissioned by the Ministry of the Interior to survey historic sites, places of scenic beauty, and natural monuments in Nara Prefecture, was chosen to supervise the preservation work. He examined and recorded features discovered during the work, including base stones and a ditch lined with dressed stone. Among other things, it was revealed that parallel to the eastern and western edge of the platform of the Great Supreme Hall were corridors running north-south; there was also reason to believe that another corridor bordered the northern edge of the platform. At the southern end of the eastern corridor lay an east-west ditch lined with cut stone. Ueda proposed that there might also have been a corridor on the southern edge, and that the Great Supreme Hall had actually been bordered on four sides by corridors.

Ueda did not suggest, however, that the Great Supreme Hall might actually be *enclosed* within a single continuous corridor. At that time, his image of the Great Supreme Hall and State Halls Compound was based firmly on the information from Heian Palace. Because there were major discrepancies between the plan at Heian Palace and the situation near Nara's Great Supreme Hall, Ueda was reluctant to accept the evidence of his own eyes at Nara. At Heian, there were corridors to the north, east, and west of the Hall, but there were no barriers between the Great Supreme Hall and the State Halls Compound to the south. There was, however, a difference in elevation between the two areas. The Great Supreme Hall was higher, resting on a stage named the Dragon Tail Platform. There was also a difference in elevation at Nara Palace where, even today, the land surface of the northern area occupied by the Great Supreme Hall is higher than that of the State Halls Compound area to the south. Ueda's predecessor Sekino superimposed his image of Heian Palace on the palace of Nara. Ueda's survey provided sufficient information to overthrow Sekino's theory, but Ueda was too cautious to leap to conclusions on the basis of what he saw as limited data.

The excavation during the summer of 1955, the first in which Nabunken carried out full-scale investigations at the Nara Palace site, was called Excavation No. 1.

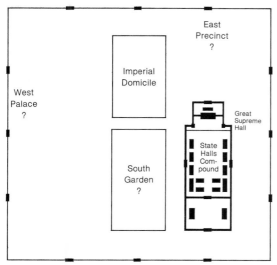

**26**
The layout of important buildings within Nara Palace as postulated by Sekino Tadashi. Sekino predicted the positioning of important palace buildings from place-names, the distribution of earthen foundation platforms at the site, paddy-field shapes, and through comparison with Heian Palace. This was the beginning of serious research on Nara Palace.

The point chosen for digging was the southern end of the eastern corridor of the Great Supreme Hall, where that corridor should have met the southern corridor, if one existed. Incidentally, during the years between Ueda's investigations and this Excavation No. 1, excavations had taken place at Fujiwara Palace, the immediate predecessor of Nara, for a period of nine years starting in 1934. As a result, the situation in the corresponding location at Fujiwara had been revealed. The Great Supreme Hall had been completely enclosed by a continuous corridor. Moreover, there was no difference in elevation between the Great Supreme Hall and State Halls Compound. Both rested directly on the land surface (which did however slope gently towards the south). When the emperor sat in the Great Supreme Hall, he did not have an unimpeded view of the myriad civil and military officials gathered in the State Halls Compound, due to the intervening corridor. For this, he would have had to leave the Great Supreme Hall and walk as far as the gate to the corridor between the Great Supreme Hall and the Twelve Halls in the State Halls Compound. Standing at the gate, moreover, the monarch would find himself on ground of nearly the same level as his subjects in the Halls. At Heian Palace, on the other hand, there was no barrier separating these two precincts. The emperor could see directly across to the Twelve Halls from his throne in the Great Supreme Hall; and since the latter building stood on higher ground than the former, he could 'look down' on his officials. What was the situation at Nara Palace? The principal goal of Excavation No. 1 was to answer this question.

There were also additional goals of a technical nature. In the planning and construction of capitals and palaces as well as of important complexes of religious buildings, it was customary to adhere strictly to rigorous standards of measurement and orientation. In trying to reconstruct the original layout of a set of buildings, it is of course necessary to determine the standards which were in effect at the time. If we are dealing, for example, with a set of facilities disposed in a left-right setting or something similar, it will be convenient first to determine the middle line between the two halves of the mirror image, and then use this as a reference point for further calculation of direction and dimensions of buildings and other features. In the case of Nara Palace as a whole, an utmost priority was to find this imaginary centre line extending north from the middle of Scarlet Phoenix Gate and bisecting the grounds. In the case of the State Halls Compound, the line sought would run from the centre of the Twelve Halls to the centre of the Great Supreme Hall, midway between the east and west corridors of the latter. Thus a second goal of Excavation No. 1 was to pinpoint and measure the location of the east and west corridors and to determine the mid-line between them.

Although it took place in average daily temperatures of 26°C, the goals of this planned twenty-day excavation were almost completely achieved within the first week. The structural relations between the Great Supreme Hall and State Halls Compound were clarified. As Ueda Sampei had supposed, a corridor was found on the south side of the Great Supreme Hall. The building had thus stood in the centre of an enclosed space circumscribed by corridors. It was also found that this area as a whole was about 1 metre higher than that on which the State Halls Compound must have stood to the south. This is very much what might have been expected from Nara Palace, standing as it did midway in time between the Fujiwara and Heian Palaces. It now became possible to reconfirm the direct line of descent, the unilinear evolution from Fujiwara Palace, built at the end of the seventh century, through the early eighth-century Nara Palace to Heian Palace, erected at the end of the eighth century (fig. 27). The researchers came to realize more clearly than ever that the ancient palaces could—indeed, must—be understood and interpreted in terms of their interrelationships within the flow of time.

With the passage of time, the structure of palace buildings changes. This is true not only for palaces in different locations—Fujiwara, Nara, Heian—but even for palaces at a single location over time. The excavation at the southeast corner of the Great Supreme Hall corridors revealed that the corridor floors were paved with volcanic tuff, and that many of the pillar base stones which lay between the paving had been made of this same yellow-grey tuff. Some of the base stones, however, were natural rocks of a dark grey granitic gneiss. The gneiss stones had clearly been laid in place of smaller tuff stones, and the surrounding paving stones had been chipped away to accommodate the larger base stones. The obvious conclusion is that, after an indeterminate period of use, the original corridor underwent repairs so extensive that even some of the base stones were replaced. It should also be remembered that the recent road-works, 300 metres to the north, had also led to the discovery that an embedded-pillar building had been replaced by a base-stone one on a single spot. During the seventy years that the capital was located here, Nara Palace underwent many changes.

The changing appearance of the Great Supreme Hall and the State Halls Compound from Fujiwara to Nara to Heian and the repeated rebuildings and renovations that took place within the Nara Palace grounds were two realities from which a new approach to Nara Palace emerged. It was to be understood not as a single still photograph but as a dynamic series of time-lapse snapshots. The image of the palace had changed radically.

The development of this new image also owed a lot to the new maps of the palace site which were made with the help of aerial photographic surveying, know as *aerial photogrammetry*. In photogrammetry, a region or an object is photographed with a special camera, and maps or scale drawings are made on the basis of the result. The photographs overlap by 60 per cent or more, and when the two overlapping pictures are viewed with the aid of a device called a plotter, a three-dimensional virtual image appears, which gives the effect of looking at the actual object or landscape. The principle is similar to that of normal vision, in which each eye presents a separate image to the brain, which then combines them. By tracing the virtual image provided by the plotter, one can produce a topographical map or scale drawing. It is also possible to take measurements from the photographs. Small objects can of course be photographed on the ground, but an aeroplane or helicopter is needed for surveying larger expanses.

Aerial photogrammetry began in France in the mid-nineteenth century, with the help of hot-air balloons. During the First World War, the Germans used the aeroplane for the same purpose, and major technical advances were made. After these war years the technique was imported into Japan. It was used by the Imperial Japanese Army's Land Survey Department, which was then in charge of producing maps of Japan, and later in Japanese-controlled Manchuria by the Manchuria Aerial Photogrammetry Company. It became the standard method for making and correcting maps. During the Allied Occupation following the Second World War, the sky was off limits to Japanese, and aerial photographic surveying in Japan was totally dependent on photographs provided by the Allied Forces. With the peace treaty of San Francisco in 1952, the skies reverted to Japan, and aerial surveying spread and developed rapidly. Almost all maps of Japan today are made with the help of this technique.

One of the first applications of this technique during its post-war revival was the mapping of the Nara Palace site. There were two reasons for this. First, the former

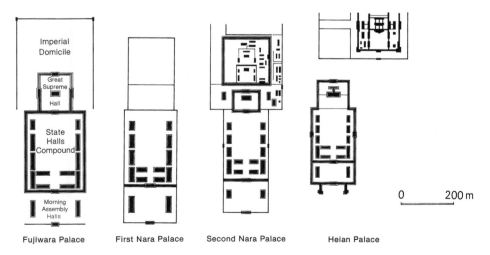

**27** Structural changes through time in the Great Supreme Hall and State Halls Compound. Around 1959, it was thought that the layout of main palace buildings had changed as shown from the seventh through the ninth centuries.

Land Survey Department became the Geographical Survey Institute (Chiri Chōsa-jo) of the Ministry of Construction. This was the predecessor of today's Geographical Survey Institute (Kokudo Chiri-in). With this development, Japanese government surveyors were finally able to import the most sophisticated post-war plotters. Discussions soon began on how to apply this powerful new tool to research projects.

Secondly, on the occasion of the national excavation project at Nara Palace in January 1954, a committee, formed to direct excavation, included among its members Fujita Ryōsaku. The archaeologist Fujita was at that time professor at Tokyo National University of Fine Arts and Music and was later to become director of Nabunken. Before and during the war, however, he had taught at Keijō Imperial University in Japanese-occupied Korea and been chief of the Korea Government-General Museum. He had gained extensive experience in excavations on the Korean Peninsula, where he came to recognize the extreme importance of having detailed maps of sites and their surroundings. It is said that Fujita urged the Nara Palace committee to produce 1:1,000 scale topographical maps of the site. The importing of the advanced new plotter was crucial to this proposal.

Nowhere in the world had such a large-scale map yet been produced by aerial photographic surveying. At a time when even maps produced by ordinary surveying techniques had only just begun to be made at a scale of 1:5,000 (for civil engineering), a 1:1,000 map was unheard of. There were therefore many technical difficulties in applying the new technology. For example, it was necessary to place elevation and position markings in the area to be mapped so that these would appear in the photographs and to decide on their optimum size and shape for a 1:1,000 map. Photographs were taken by a private company from a height of 1,650 metres, using a Zeiss RMK 21/28 aerial camera. The resulting photos were on a scale of approximately 1:7,500. With the help of the plotter, a 1:1,000 map of the Nara Palace site was completed.

During the 1955 excavation, the researchers staying with the Mizobe family, who had long been active in the preservation of the palace site, gathered around the newly completed 1:1,000 map and discussed various aspects of the situation.

It was agreed that the palace had obviously been extended, rebuilt, and repaired at various times. Moreover, it was noted that at the site of the present excavation at the southeast corner of the corridor surrounding the Great Supreme Hall very few of the roof tiles and pottery seemed to belong to the years around 710 when the palace was built. The archaeologists all agreed that on stylistic grounds the tiles seemed to date from the middle of the century or later. The tiles found in the region of the Great Supreme Hall podium, which were presumably from the roof of that building, were also identical to these. In that case, was it right to continue to accept Sekino Tadashi's assumption that the Great Supreme Hall Compound and the State Halls Compound to the south dated from the time of the palace's establishment?

Looking at the 1:1,000 map with such doubts in mind, it had to be remembered that the Great Supreme Hall and State Halls Compound were located in the eastern half of the palace grounds. Was it not strange that these building complexes, which played a central role in palace events, were not located on the centre line of the grounds? At both Fujiwara and Heian, they were right in the centre. Looking at the 1:1,000 topographical map again, at the area just inside and directly in line with Scarlet Phoenix Gate, one could detect amidst the farmlands a raised platform and several long, narrow fields, a pattern, in fact, that seemed to mirror that of the Great Supreme Hall and State Halls Compound just to the east. Sekino had seen here a resemblance to the Hall of Prosperity and Happiness, a banquet hall at Heian Palace. So he equated the area with Nara's South Garden (see fig. 26), which is mentioned in written sources. But there is also a clear resemblance to the State Halls Compound to the east. Cannot we equally well designate *this* area as the State Halls Compound? In that case, would it not make sense that these centrally located buildings were the original Great Supreme Hall and State Halls Compound from the time of the palace's creation, and that the eastward buildings now under excavation were a second Great Supreme Hall and State Halls Compound built some time later?

The *Shoku Nihongi* chronicle recounts that when the capital was moved to Kuni in 740, the Great Supreme Hall and corridors at Nara Palace were disassembled and rebuilt at Kuni. The capital returned to Nara in 745, and an entry for the year 749 refers once again to the Great Supreme Hall in Nara Palace. Therefore the hall and the State Halls Compound are assumed to have been rebuilt between 745 and 749. The buildings in the eastern part of the palace grounds must have been the rebuilt ones. The hypothetical dating of the roof tiles of the eastern area also supported this assumption. What then was the situation concerning further building activity at the Great Supreme Hall corridor, which we had just finished excavating? In the *Shoku Nihongi*, an entry from 761 notes: 'Since the new palace was not yet completed, the New Year's Morning Ceremony was cancelled.' Apparently some sort of rebuilding was under way. Perhaps we could equate this phase of construction with the renovation of the corridor which is reflected in the change of base stones.

Using our map to measure the east-west width of the first, original State Halls Compound, we find it to be about 215 metres. At Fujiwara this dimension was 225 metres, for the second Nara building, 185 metres, and at Heian, 160 metres. The State Halls Compound had thus become progressively narrower. On the basis of width, our putative original Nara State Halls Compound takes its expected place within the series. To the researchers assembled around the new map, this was further reason to consider a new working hypothesis: that there had been two successive Great Supreme Halls and two successive State Halls Compounds at Nara Palace.

In contrast to the State Halls Compound, the Great Supreme Hall grew steadily wider from Fujiwara to Nara to Heian. The emperor's audience hall grew larger as his officials' quarters shrank; the audience hall was raised to a higher level than the officials' precinct; and the emperor could view ceremonies and events taking place in the State Halls Compound without leaving his seat in the Great Supreme Hall. These developments surely reflect a change in the emperor's status.

With the completion of Excavation No. 1 at Nara Palace in 1955, digging at the site was suspended for four years as Nabunken researchers turned their attention to the Asuka region in southern Nara Prefecture. This was a forced decision because a new irrigation ditch to serve the Nara Basin was to cut through the Asuka region, and it was necessary to do a preliminary survey of archaeological sites in the area to provide data for planning the ditch's course. This was the first time the archaeologist's trowel had seriously broken earth in the famed Asuka region, rich in the remains and rumours of ancient buildings: Asuka-dera, Japan's oldest fully-fledged Buddhist temple erected in the late sixth century; Kawara-dera, built in the mid-seventh century in the Chinese Tang style; Asuka-Itabuki Palace, one of several seventh-century palaces, whose location was recorded although the remains discovered at that location had not yet been identified with the palace.

During these four years, however, the situation at Nara Palace did not remain unchanged. Work had been completed on the widening of the road generally known as 1st Row Road, which passed through the northern part of the designated Special Historic Site (see p. 43). Following this, there were repeated applications for permission to erect new buildings alongside the newly-widened road. Official approval must be received before carrying out any new construction or alterations to existing buildings within a Historic Site. Once an application is received, permission may not be granted for as much as a year, while the necessary small-scale archaeological excavation is conducted. There were complaints from those who could not understand why there were such obstacles to building on their own land. Many saw these obstacles as a violation of property rights, and it was perhaps only to be expected that in January 1959, at a residents' meeting in Saki-chō, it was decided to form a Subcommittee to Promote the Cancellation of the Historic Site Designation. The prefectural Board of Education, the body in charge of administering Historic Sites, hastened to find a satisfactory solution. In order to evaluate the flood of applications on the basis of their effect on cultural properties, it was necessary to understand the overall subsurface situation. This would require extensive and continuous excavations. After fierce debate, the residents agreed to co-operate in the archaeological investigations and await the results. Excavations at Nara Palace were resumed in 1959.

Given the number of applications for building permits along 1st Row Road, it was decided to begin the new excavations there. To avoid the problems involved in leasing private land, an on-site office was set up on public land about 150 metres to the northeast of the second Great Supreme Hall, and Excavation No. 3 was begun in April 1960.

In the area chosen for excavation, Ueda Sampei had already in 1924 confirmed the presence of two base stones and a podium. What structure might this represent? The Nabunken staff, with the image of the two Great Supreme Halls in their minds, was now puzzled over the identity of this feature lying just to the north of the second Great Supreme Hall Compound, as well as over the identity of the mammoth building further to the north whose traces had been discovered during the 1954 road-works (see p. 46). There was also the question of the location of the Imperial Domicile. Excavation No. 3 provided some answers.

The area excavated was a mere 8.7 ares, but the remains of an unusual corridor running north-south were discovered on its eastern edge. Previously known corridors typically had either two parallel rows of pillars to support the roof, or three rows. In the latter case, the pillars of the middle row supported the ridgepole and

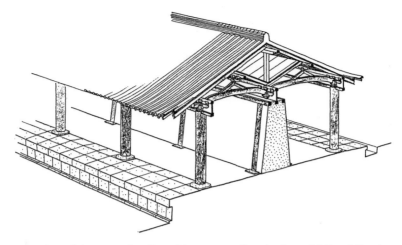

**28** Reconstruction of the tamped-wall corridor surrounding the Imperial Domicile. Around the Imperial Domicile ran a specially constructed barrier consisting of a central tamped-earth wall with covered pathways down both sides.

were connected by thin (less than 30 centimetres) tamped-earth walls with lattice windows, so that there were two separate corridors. The corridor of Excavation No. 3 was of this double-corridor type, but it was unusual in that its tamped-earth dividing wall was some 1.5 metres thick, while each corridor had a width of 3 metres or more. Because of the imposing thickness of the dividing earthen wall, such structures are termed 'tamped-wall corridors' (fig. 28). Just such a corridor surrounded the Imperial Domicile at Heian Palace, so it might be supposed that the one at Nara had also enclosed the emperor's residence. The base stones found in 1954 in connection with the mammoth building to the north might then represent the northern side of the corridor. If we consider together Ueda's records for 1924, the 1954 find, and the results of Excavation No. 3, it appears that the area enclosed by the corridor—probably the Imperial Domicile—was 176.9 metres east to west and 185.3 metres north to south and sat nicely to the north of the second Great Supreme Hall. Subsequent excavation, in fact, revealed evidence of a feature, within the square formed by the corridor, which seemed a reasonable indication of the Imperial Domicile. Thus it appeared that the second Nara Palace Great Supreme Hall was bracketed by the Imperial Domicile to the north and the State Halls Compound to the south, forming one large unit. The same situation presumably obtained with the first Great Supreme Hall. Our hypothetical image of the layout of the palace gradually came into clearer focus: in the centre of the grounds, the original grouping of the Imperial Domicile, Great Supreme Hall, and State Halls Compound; to its east, a second similar grouping. For convenience, we can speak of these two phases in the history of the palace as 'the first Nara Palace' and 'the second Nara Palace'. Perhaps we might also now name this image as a whole the 'two-palace theory'.

In the light of this hypothesis of the first and second palaces, synthesized from the evidence of features and of the 1:1,000 map, another fact was of particular interest.

During the excavations at Scarlet Phoenix Gate described above (pp. 36–38), it emerged that at some time the gate fell into disuse and was demolished. On the podium, near its northern edge, there are traces of a row of square pillars 20 centimetres on a side which must date from after the gate's abandonment. It is thought that these pillars are evidence that a fence was built to seal off the former gate. When was the gate abandoned and blockaded? Archaeology provides no conclusive data. There are only two references to Scarlet Phoenix Gate in the *Shoku Nihongi* chronicle. It is recorded that ceremonies were held before the gate in 715 and 734. The lack of later references may be fortuitous, since references to *any* of the palace gates are rare. Nevertheless, consider this passage from 740. 'It has been four years since the Great Supreme Hall and corridors of Nara were pulled down to be rebuilt at Kuni Palace.' If Scarlet Phoenix Gate was also included in the move to Kuni Palace, then the recently discovered fence takes on great significance. There is no trace of the gate having been rebuilt on the same site after its demolition. When the capital moved back to Nara in 745 and the main palace buildings were reconstructed to the east of their original location, is it possible that Scarlet Phoenix Gate was not rebuilt?

It should also be remembered that in the second Nara Palace, the gate which would have been equivalent to a main gate, directly south of the State Halls Compound, was the eastern gate of the south Great Wall. In the *Shoku Nihongi* entry for the fifth month of 768 we find this gate referred to as Naka-no-Mibu Gate. In all cases except at Nara, the eastern south gate is called simply Mibu Gate. Could it be that the word *naka*—'middle'—had been prefixed to indicate this gate's adopted role as the main palace gate? After the main palace buildings were moved eastward, this gate must have usurped the function of Scarlet Phoenix Gate. To the investigators this seemed to constitute independent confirmation of the two-palace theory.

In May 1962 a major report entitled *Nara Imperial Palace: Archaeological Surveys Carried Out in 1959–1961* was released by Nabunken (Publications no. 15). At the time of this report, the investigators held the following view of the relocation and rebuilding of the main palace buildings.

When Nara Palace was founded, the Imperial Domicile, Great Supreme Hall, and State Halls Compound were aligned north to south in the centre of the palace grounds. The area to the east may have been occupied by the East Palace, residence of the crown prince. One theory was that when the capital returned to Nara in 745, after sojourns in Kuni, Shigaraki, and Naniwa, the Imperial Domicile, Great Supreme Hall, and State Halls Compound were rebuilt to the east of their original positions. An alternative theory was that when Empress Kōken ascended the throne in 749, she had her own Great Supreme Hall and State Halls Compound built to the east of the original site, directly in front of the East Palace that had been her residence as crown princess. In either case, there was no evidence that a new set of offices was erected on the original site after the move to the eastern area. At Heian Palace, the State Halls Compound stood in the centre of the palace grounds, and to its west was a banquet hall of almost the same size, the Hall of Prosperity and Happiness. It was possible, the 1962 report suggested, that increasing specialization during the Nara period led to the original site of Nara Palace's Great Supreme Hall and related buildings being converted to a function similar to that of Heian's Hall of Prosperity and Happiness.

## Verification of hypotheses through excavation

The two-palace theory now seemed secure. At the same time, the state of affairs surrounding the excavation was undergoing a dramatic transformation. In 1962, when the report was published, the staff at Nabunken numbered only twenty-three; of these, thirteen were researchers and the other ten were administrative workers. These numbers were to change drastically. The stimulus was the need to preserve the Nara Palace site.

The Nara Palace site lies a mere 30 minutes from Osaka and Kyoto. In 1960 a Joint Security Treaty was signed by Japan and the United States, and Prime Minister Ikeda announced his plan for doubling per capita income within ten years. With the opening of the Tokyo Olympics in 1964, Japan seemed to have put the post-war era well behind her. The northern Nara Basin, home of the ancient Nara Capital, was rapidly changing from a farming district to a dense residential area oriented towards the big cities of Osaka and Kyoto. The private Kinki Nippon Railway Company (better known as Kintetsu) that carried this new population to Osaka and Kyoto needed to build additional storage and inspection facilities for their rolling stock. The location that they chose lay within the Nara Palace site.

At that time, the eastern two-thirds of the site had been designated a Special Historic Site (not including the eastern projection, which had not yet been discovered), but the western third was being treated no differently from any other non-designated area. The Kintetsu railway company planned to build its facilities in the southern part of this western third of the site. The CPCP took the view that land on non-designated areas was free to be sold and developed, as long as any archaeological features or artifacts discovered in the course of construction were duly reported. Thus the CPCP in February 1963 gave permission for Kintetsu to begin construction.

Many people, however, were disturbed by these plans. Excavations at the palace site had reaped an unexpectedly impressive crop in the few short years of continuous excavation. The western third may have been non-designated, but there was now every reason to suspect that it too held important archaeological materials. There was also a feeling that the Nara Palace site should be preserved as a unit. It would hardly do to cut off parts of it here and there. When the *Asahi Shimbun*, Japan's largest newspaper, carried a report on the railway construction question, voices were raised throughout the country demanding the preservation of the site. The issue was even debated in the Diet. Faced with this deluge of opposition, the CPCP had little choice but to rescind permission for construction and support the preservation of the palace as a whole. As part of a three-year plan beginning in 1963, it was determined that the government should buy up all remaining private land within the site. Nara Palace entered a new era.

With the onset of this new era, policy towards excavation was also re-examined. In April 1963 the Heijō (=Nara) Palace Site Research Department was established within Nabunken, and plans were laid to excavate the entire site over a twelve-year period. In conjunction with these plans, the regular staff at Nabunken was expanded to twenty-nine in 1963, fifty in 1964, and fifty-nine in 1965. The number of researchers alone was more than quadrupled. In the course of this expansion, young archaeologists, architectural historians, and historians were recruited from all over Japan.

'New minds bring new ideas.' The new recruits found themselves involved immediately in the series of excavations which, although intended to outline the four sides of the rectangular palace grounds, instead led to the discovery of the palace's eastern extension (see pp. 23–30). Thus, from the beginning their work involved them in the questioning of past theories. Even the two-palace theory, which to the older researchers was still a bright new idea whose veracity they themselves had confirmed, was to the new recruits just another old theory needing re-examination.

One of the grounds for accepting the two-palace theory was the researchers' opinion of the dating of roof tiles from the eastern complex of the second palace. A unique type of eave tile had been used in the second State Halls Compound and Great Supreme Hall. At Nabunken, artifacts were designated according to their type by the use of four-digit numbers. When finer classifications were needed, a single alphabetic character was appended. In such numerical terms, the unique eave tiles of the second palace were designated Type 6225 for round eave tiles and Type 6663 for 'flat' eave tiles (fig. 29 *left*). In terms of the research done on roof tiles up to that time, it was thought that neither of these types could have dated from the time of the foundation of Nara Palace, that is, they must date from no earlier than the end of the 740s. Furthermore, since the second Imperial Domicile was considered to form a unit with the second Great Supreme Hall and State Halls Compound, it was assumed that its own unique eave tiles, Types 6311 (round) and 6664 (flat), must also date from that period (fig. 29 *right*). This also seemed reasonable from the viewpoint of typological studies. Doubts about the two-palace theory arose in the first instance from doubts about the dating of the roof tiles.

The continuing excavations along modern-day 1st Row Road, begun in 1959, had reached the northern edge of the second Imperial Domicile by 1962–64. At this time a fact which was relevant to the dating of the roof tiles came to light. In a pit 3.5 metres square and 40 centimetres deep, excavators found not only eave tiles of Types 6311 and 6664 but also some wooden tablets. The pit also contained large quantities of scraps of wood and of cypress bark of the type used for roofing. This was most likely a rubbish pit in use during construction (cf. fig. 35).

The pit contained 111 wooden tablets in all. Four of these were dated either 728 or 729. If these tablets were labels for provisions of some sort, it is possible that the goods were stored for a period of years before being utilized, and then the wooden labels were thrown away. In such a case, the dates on the tablets would most likely not correspond to the year in which they were tossed into the rubbish pit. However, one of these tablets, dated 729, was a delivery tag attached to a consignment of special metal door fittings being sent to a certain bureau. On its back is what appears to be a signature indicating receipt of the goods. Since these door fittings were apparently quite special, and since no other goods are listed in the consignment, it can be assumed that the delivered goods would have been used almost immediately and the tablet would then have been thrown away. Accordingly, this rubbish pit was probably being used by 729 or soon after. The pit also yielded other tablets pertaining to the delivery of metal fittings and lumber for construction.

This pit, with its wooden tablets and its eave tiles, was covered by a layer of dirt 60 to 70 centimetres thick. Yet another pit had been dug into this dirt layer; from its position closer to the surface, this second pit was obviously more recent in date than the lower one. The second pit also contained tablets, two of which bore the dates 746 and 750 respectively. We can therefore presume that it was a rubbish pit in use around that time. The dates on the tablets in these two pits correspond nicely with their relative stratigraphy.

Accepting the above conclusions about the dating of these two pits, we can also conclude that the artifacts recovered from the lower pit were presumably manufactured before, or not much later than, 729. But among these artifacts were eave tiles of Types 6311 and 6664, used at the Imperial Domicile of the second palace. It appears, then, that the second Imperial Domicile could not have been erected after about 730. It must be older. In that case, the second Great Supreme Hall and State Halls Compound should also be older, and it would appear likely that the central and eastern complexes, so alike in scale and structure, actually coexisted for a period of time.

According to the two-palace theory, the major buildings of the second palace are assumed to have been built in the late 740s. The new information about the dating of the roof tiles of the second Imperial Domicile, based on the contents of the trash pit, clearly contradict this assumption. The theory began to look shaky. In order to support the theory, or to propose a new one to replace it, we could only await new information from continued excavation.

Excavation at the site of the second Imperial Domicile, which began in 1960, had by 1973 almost entirely revealed its eastern half, thus giving us a fairly complete picture of the area. As for the buildings to the south, no work had been done at the second Great Supreme Hall since the exploration of its southeast corridor corner in

**29** Sets of eave tiles. Eave tile Types 6225 (round) and 6663 (flat) were used in the second State Halls Compound (*left*), while Types 6311 (round) and 6664 (flat) were used in the second Imperial Domicile (*right*).

1955, and the State Halls Compound had lain untouched since the 1968 excavation at the East Morning Assembly Hall. Excavations were resumed in 1978 at the Great Supreme Hall and have continued to the present. Excavation in the central area of the palace grounds had been sporadic since the 1964 digging near Scarlet Phoenix Gate. Since 1970, however, annual excavation has continued and has now exposed almost all of the eastern half of the central area. This series of excavations spanning two decades is in the process of producing a new image of the Imperial Domicile, Great Supreme Hall, and State Halls Compound (figs. 30, 33). However, certain areas remain almost totally uninvestigated, in particular, the second State Halls Compound. For this reason, it is too early to reach firm conclusions. Nevertheless, let us sum up the present-day view of the situation at Nara Palace, freely incorporating conjectures as necessary to complete the picture.

In the year 708, at Fujiwara Palace, Empress Genmei announced that the capital would be moved to Nara. Construction began on the new palace and capital. At the palace, work began, slightly north of dead centre of the grounds, on the Great Supreme Hall Compound with the Great Supreme Hall at its heart. Figure 31 shows a tentative reconstruction of the situation. The compound, surrounded by a tamped-wall corridor (cf. fig. 28), measured 176.6 metres east-west and 317.7 metres north-south; in terms of the measuring system of the time, this corresponded to 500 by 900 'large *shaku*'.* In the centre of the south face of the corridor was a gate. This gate was positioned at the exact centre of the entire palace grounds. Entering the Great Supreme Hall Compound through this gate, one would come upon a wide, gravelled plaza, covering some 3.5 hectares. A path 40 metres wide extended from the gate through the centre of the plaza. The plaza covered the entire southern two-thirds of the area enclosed by the tamped-wall corridor. The northern third was raised 2.2 metres higher than the plaza. The southern face of this earthen terrace was reinforced by a brick wall (fig. 32). The bricks used here weighed 5 to 6 kilograms and were approximately 30 × 15 × 7.5 centimetres, that is, 1 *shaku* by 5 *sun* by 2.5 *sun*. More than 16,000 bricks were used in the wall. To ascend the terrace, one would use one of the ramps that lay to its right and left, just inside and parallel to the corridor. The centre of the terrace was occupied by a large building whose podium measured 53 metres east-west by 29.5 metres north-south. Only a few vestiges of stone remained on the podium perimeter and the stairways that ascended to it. The building on its top—presumably the Great Supreme Hall— would have had an area of about 900 square metres. Behind this building stood the slightly smaller Rear Hall.

What evidence can we adduce for identifying this large building as the Great Supreme Hall? First, it is a large-scale structure, directly in line with Scarlet Phoenix Gate. A second point is its relation with the Great Supreme Hall at Kuni Palace. As mentioned above, the *Shoku Nihongi* chronicle reports that Nara's Great Supreme Hall was later moved to Kuni Capital. Besides this building, there is one more candidate for identification as a Great Supreme Hall: the one we have con-

---

*At that time there were two sizes of *shaku*, the large *shaku* being equal to 1.2 small *shaku*; large *shaku* were used only in measuring land. However, the large *shaku* almost immediately went out of use, and all subsequent measurements were calculated in terms of (small) *shaku*.

sidered as belonging to the second Nara Palace, whose platform survives to the east and has long been called Great Supreme Hall by local residents. This platform was finally excavated in 1978, and excavations of the Great Supreme Hall at Kuni were completed in 1977. Comparing these three buildings, it turns out that the putative second Great Supreme Hall at Nara is smaller than the one at Kuni, as determined both by the size of its platform and by the spacing of its pillars. It would hardly seem possible to dismantle a building and then reassemble it on the same basic plan using the same lumber, yet have it come out smaller. The building which we have tentatively called the first Great Supreme Hall at Nara matches the size of the one at Kuni much more closely. This is a further point in favour of the identification.

Abutting the Great Supreme Hall Compound on the south was a precinct measuring 600 large *shaku* (284 metres) east-west and 800 large *shaku* (314 metres) north-south. It was surrounded by a board fence with embedded pillars. This fence stood on a podium about 70 centimetres high. The pillars were quite thick—45 centimetres in diameter—and were spaced about 3 metres apart. Apparent remnants of these pillars reveal that after the wall was torn down, the pillars were hollowed out and used as part of an underground water conduit. If we are correct in identifying this section of conduit as one of the pillars of the fence, then we can conclude that each pillar was originally sunk about 2.5 metres into the soil and projected as much as 5.7 metres above ground including the roof, an imposing barrier indeed!

Although this board-fence precinct was probably included in the original plans for the palace, construction was apparently not completed until the late 720s. A gate in the south side of the fence faced towards Scarlet Phoenix Gate. Unlike the rest of the fence, it seems to have been a base-stone structure with a podium. Entering this gate, one would find four long, narrow buildings, two on each side in a perfect north-south alignment (see fig. 33 *left*). These were base-stone buildings with podia. In each case the shorter, east-west dimension was spanned by five

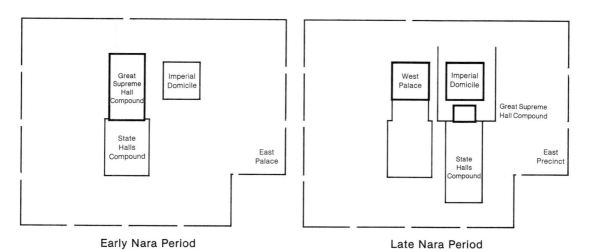

Early Nara Period                              Late Nara Period

**30** Changes in the central compounds of Nara Palace. The layout of the central Nara Palace compounds is estimated to have changed as shown between the early and late Nara period; however, there is as yet no archaeological confirmation of this shift.

pillars separated uniformly by 11 *shaku*. On their long sides, the two northern buildings had eleven pillars spaced 15 *shaku* apart, while the two southern buildings had twenty-two pillars with the same spacing. The distance between the northern and southern buildings was 50 *shaku*. The unit used here was the usual 'small *shaku*', the one always used in architecture, measuring 29.3 centimetres. The total length of the two buildings on each side (including the 50 *shaku* between them) was therefore nearly 160 metres. This fenced compound, with two large buildings to either side and a long open space through its middle, is generally identified with the State Halls Compound.

While the Great Supreme Hall was being built, construction was also proceeding on the Imperial Domicile to the east—at what was formerly thought to be the site of the *second* Imperial Domicile. The building was enclosed by a sturdy, embedded-pillar wooden fence which measured 500 large *shaku* on each side. The distance between this enclosure and that of the Great Supreme Hall to the west was 300 large *shaku*. Within the enclosure, the buildings in which the imperial family would live began to take shape. Construction activities continued even after the buildings were finished. For example, at some time the fence was rebuilt and the compound was extended to the south.

The buildings of the Great Supreme Hall and State Halls Compound were almost totally tile-roofed, base-stone pillar structures. The pillars of the Imperial Domicile, by contrast, were almost all embedded, and although a few portions of the roofs were tiled, the most of the roof area was covered with shingles of board or of cypress bark. The base-stone tile-roofed type of building was imported from the continent at the end of the sixth century, as a style of temple architecture; but the embedded-pillar shingled building had been present in Japan from much earlier. Since they were the sites for public activities such as ceremonies and political business, the Great Supreme Hall and State Halls Compound were built on the continental model. As a private space for the activities of daily family life, however, the imperial family evidently preferred the traditional style of building.

Construction was completed for the present in the central area of the palace grounds. Entering Scarlet Phoenix Gate, one would first see a path of some 250 metres which ended before a precinct demarcated by a high fence. Through the gate of this precinct, to the left and right, were the long buildings of the State Halls Compound, where high-ranking officials gathered each morning for the performance of their duties. To the north was a separate walled precinct, the Great Supreme Hall Compound, where the emperor would come each morning from his dwelling to the east. Officials would enter this compound for their Morning Obeisance to the emperor or when they had something to report. When speaking, they would look up to the emperor on his terrace from the gravelled plaza.

The layout of the Great Supreme Hall and State Halls Compound differs radically from what is known of Fujiwara, Naniwa, Nagaoka, and Heian Palaces. The State Halls Compound at Fujiwara, Naniwa, and Heian consisted of twelve buildings, six each to the east and west as opposed to the four buildings at Nara. (At Nagaoka, there were four on each side for a total of eight.) Remember that the State Halls Compound was also called the Twelve Halls. Normally another pair of buildings, the Morning Assembly Halls, stood directly to the south of the State

**31** Reconstructed appearance of the first Great Supreme Hall.

**32** Remains of the brick wall reinforcing the southern terrace of the first Great Supreme Hall. The front face of this terrace was dressed with bricks, a feature not seen at other palaces.

Halls Compound. The officials would stop here on their way to their seats in the State Halls Compound each morning, to change into Morning Dress and perform their toilette. At Nara, these buildings were absent. The Great Supreme Hall precinct, too, is distinctive at Nara. Elsewhere, it gives the feeling of being an appendage to the State Halls Compound. At Nara, it is unusually large and is given special treatment through, for example, the liberal use of bricks.

The relocation of the capital to Kuni in 740 wrought great changes at Nara. The Great Supreme Hall Compound was rebuilt at Kuni, and its tamped-wall corridor was replaced by a wooden fence at Nara. The south gate of the State Halls Compound was blockaded by a wooden barrier. As mentioned earlier, it may also be that the Scarlet Phoenix Gate was dismantled at this time and blockaded by a fence. But after a brief span of five years at Kuni, Shigaraki, and Naniwa, the capital returned to Nara. Rebuilding and renovation now began on a grand scale. There were also major changes within the imperial family. In 748 the retired Empress Genshō died, and the following year Emperor Shōmu abdicated in favour of his daughter Abe (Empress Kōken). Surely the extensive renovations also reflect these events.

The former Great Supreme Hall Compound in the north centre of the palace grounds maintained its east-west width, but its length diminished from 317.7 to 186 metres. Major changes also took place within its confines (fig. 33). The high barrier of bricks south of the Great Supreme Hall was buried, as the terrace was extended southward some 18 metres into the plaza. An orderly collection of embedded-pillar buildings, perhaps some thirty in all, was erected on the terrace. The pillars were spaced regularly throughout at a distance of 10 *shaku*. The eaves of neighbouring buildings formed a continuum, and two large buildings might be linked by a

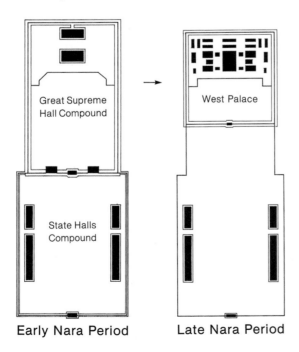

**Early Nara Period**        **Late Nara Period**

*33*
Changes in the buildings of the central area of Nara Palace. The central area, which at first consisted of the Great Supreme Hall and State Halls Compound, was transformed into space for the imperial family residence in the north and facilities for entertaining in the south.

smaller building. The result was a series of building complexes, each constituting a large living space, so that one could pass from building to building without actually going outside. The four huge buildings remained at the State Halls Compound, but the surrounding wooden fence was replaced by a tamped-wall corridor. It is possible that these buildings lost their original function. As for Scarlet Phoenix Gate, there is no evidence of its having been rebuilt.

Over to the east, equally important alterations were under way (see fig. 30 *right*), not unconnected with the changes in the central area. The wooden fence around the Imperial Domicile was replaced by a tamped-wall corridor, perhaps more in keeping with the expected aura of dignity. To the south, a new Great Supreme Hall and State Halls Compound were established. Unlike the original State Halls Compound, this second one had twelve halls and a pair of Morning Assembly Halls to its south. A revival of the Fujiwara Palace pattern, perhaps? The buildings in this eastern area are the ones assumed from long ago to have been the original and only Great Supreme Hall and State Halls Compound at Nara Palace.

The eastern Imperial Domicile had been upgraded. In the north-central area of the grounds, meanwhile, there was an impressive array of buildings which appeared to be dwellings. Both of these complexes were imposing enough to have served as residences for the imperial family. Considering that this was a period when both the current ruler and the immediate predecessor were often living in the palace simultaneously—retired Emperor Shōmu and Empress Kōken, then Empress Kōken and her successor Emperor Junnin—it is hardly surprising that there should have been two such dwelling areas. These areas are probably the Middle Palace and West Palace (fig. 34) of contemporary written sources.

**34** Excavation of the West Palace. In the northern portion of the central palace area—the suspected location of the West Palace—numerous postholes were excavated in orderly alignment.

The excavations in the central area of the palace site had borne impressive fruit. The conception of two successive Nara Palaces, one with its major buildings in the centre of the grounds and the other having them to the east, had been held since the beginning of full-scale excavations at the site. With the continuous digging, this view had now been rectified and fleshed out with concrete data. The two-palace theory, which at one time looked as if it would need to be discarded altogether, seems to be regaining credibility, albeit in a different guise. It is as if a stationary pendulum, after a major disturbance, was returning to its centre. But the question has by no means been resolved for all time.

The interpretation presented above of the history of construction of the major palace buildings is not shared by all investigators; alternative hypotheses abound. For example, it was mentioned above (pp. 62, 64) that the original Great Supreme Hall and State Halls Compound are quite out of conformity with those at other palaces. Some take the view that this was not a State Halls Compound at all but from the beginning was intended as some sort of banquet facility, rather like the Hall of Prosperity and Happiness at Heian Palace.

At present, excavations are continuing in the area to the east usually identified as the second State Halls Compound. The large platform which remains on the surface today was presumably laid after the capital reverted to Nara in 745, but excavation of the layer *below* the surface has begun to reveal a group of embedded-pillar buildings of a type similar to the State Halls Compound. What was the function of these buildings, and when were they erected? As one investigator put it, 'The more we dig, the less we understand.' Perhaps this feeling is inevitable for those actually participating in on-site investigations. The results of each excavation lead to a re-evaluation of previous theories and the re-examination of past data. Even with archaeological data, seemingly so solid and concrete, one occasionally finds oneself doubting whether the situation could really have been as described in the original excavation report. It may even be necessary at times to re-excavate a site. Each new excavation poses new riddles and calls for new hypotheses.

# Chapter 3

# Writing, Wooden Tablets, and Ceramics

### The discovery of the first wooden tablet

It was a cold January 1961, with the average daily temperature in Nara a mere 2.5 °C. Excavation No. 5, begun the previous November, was in its final stages. The excavation was being carried out on the north side of the existing road known as 1st Row Road. In those days when we were not yet aware of the existence of the eastern extension, this location was supposed to be a little to the north of the exact centre of the palace grounds. One of the last remaining tasks was to dig to the bottom of a pit we had discovered and to search for artifacts. On 24 January, under a light snowfall, Tanaka, his assistant Terada Sōken, and a few other excavators were at work in this pit, which was later to be given the reference number SK219. For several days, the pit had been yielding a wealth of potsherds as well as cypress bark roofing materials and pieces of wood (cf. fig. 35). On a few of the sherds were characters written in China ink. Since at that time we were concentrating our efforts on researching the artifacts from Nara Palace, which included mostly earthenwares and roof tiles, we expected to learn much from the excavation of this particular pit. At about 2 P.M., Terada called out that he had found something that looked like writing. On the fragment of wood that rested in his palm, still submerged in the muddy water of a bucket, writing could indeed be seen. This was the first wooden tablet (*mokkan*) to be discovered on the site.

If you were to ask me (Tanaka) what has been the biggest change in the excavation situation at Nara Palace between 1955, when full-scale digging began, and the present, I would answer without hesitation: the discovery of the wooden tablets. In the research into the naming of the gates of the Great Wall described in the previous chapter, tablets with gate names written on them played a major role. Tablets with dates inscribed on them provided many clues for determining the chronology of the principal palace buildings. That roof tiles and pottery can be useful in fixing the chronology of features is only possible because ceramics with the same characteristics have been found elsewhere in conjunction with dated wooden tablets. It would be impossible to tell the tale of the excavation and research at Nara Palace and Nara Capital without devoting part of the narrative to these *mokkan*.

So far, more than 135,000 tablets have been found at Nara Palace (pl. 5) and Nara Capital. Among them, 25,000 tablets have already been catalogued and published, and they may be roughly classified according to their written content. First, there are correspondence, records, and ledgers pertaining to official clerical business within the governmental bureaux; secondly, there are shipping labels for tribute goods coming into the capital from the provinces; thirdly, there are invent-ory tags for identifying goods in storage; and finally, there are tablets bearing ran-dom scribblings, graffiti, penmanship practice, and so forth. As for their shape, tablets used mainly for official correspondence and record-keeping tend to be rect-angular strips, while shipping and inventory tags either may be pointed at one end to allow them to be easily inserted into the wrapping material, or may have indenta-tions at either end so that they might be bound together with string. Most of the tablets discovered in excavations were those that had been tossed away after their usefulness had lapsed. Less than a fourth retained their original shape or were com-plete enough to allow that shape to be reconstructed. About 15 per cent had either their upper or lower half intact, while another 35 per cent, which could be identified as *mokkan* by split and planed surfaces and/or the existence of characters, were so damaged that their original shape could not be known. Being made of wood, the tablets could be re-used over and over by shaving the writing surface clean. About 25 per cent of tablet remains consist of such shavings—which of course often bear writing (fig. 36).

Some fifteen years after the discovery of the first *mokkan* on the Nara Palace ground, I (Tanaka) came across Robin Birley's book, *Vindolanda: A Roman Frontier Post on Hadrian's Wall* (London, 1977), describing the excavations at that site in northern England. Reading through it, I discovered that there were 'wooden writing tablets' in Vindolanda as well. These dated from the Roman Empire of the late first century A.D. and had been discovered in 1973. Researchers in Japan were aware of the existence of wooden tablets in ancient China and of inscribed white birch-bark tablets from ancient Russia—but in western Europe? The situation sur-rounding the discovery at Vindolanda closely resembled that of the discovery of the

**35** Rubbish heap. Ancient rubbish heaps are mountains of treasures for archaeologists. At Nara Capital as well, organic materials which usually decompose and disappear have survived very well in deep rubbish pits. This photograph illustrates the condition of a trash deposit in a dis-used well.

first *mokkan* so far away at Nara Palace. There were also points of resemblance to the ancient Japanese tablets themselves, and of course great differences. For example, the writing on the Roman tablets had been done in ink with a reed pen, whereas in Japan a brush and China ink was used. The Roman examples were mostly between 1 and 3 millimetres thick, and some were even less than a milli-metre, while the Japanese ones were much thicker, averaging about 5 millimetres. In terms of content, the main difference was the presence at Vindolanda of several examples of longer correspondences, including personal letters; none such have been found in Japan. Conversely, the shipping and inventory labels so numerous in Japan seem to be unknown among the Roman examples. Such comparisons promise to be interesting.

To return to Pit SK219, of the forty tablets recovered, four were dated: a label dated to what we believe is the fifth year of Tempyō Hōji, or A.D. 761, which accom-panied a tax shipment of salt from Hidaka County, Kii Province (modern Wakayama Prefecture); two labels which accompanied a tax shipment of walnuts from Yamanashi County, Kai Province (Yamanashi Prefecture) in 762; and a dating corresponding to 762 found on a shaving produced in preparing a tablet for re-use. In examining the ceramic contents unearthed from Pit SK219, it was found that potsherds from the bottom and top of the pit could be identified as belonging to the same vessel. This is evidence that the pit was probably in use for only a very brief period. Presumably broken pottery, useless *mokkan*, wood scraps and the like were tossed into the hole and then covered over almost immediately. The condition of the soil within the pit is not inconsistent with this surmise. When exactly, then, was it filled in?

Of the four dated tablets in the pit, three were shipping tags for tax goods. (The original function of the fourth, which survives only as a shaving, is unknown.) If

**36** Shavings from wooden tablets. By shaving down the face of *mokkan*, they could be re-used several times. Such shavings have been unearthed in great quantities.

the tax goods—salt and walnuts—were consumed as soon as they arrived at Nara Palace and the tags immediately thrown away, then the dates on these tablets would be close to the date at which the pit was filled in. Unfortunately, we do not know whether the goods were used immediately. If they were stored with the tags still attached and then only later removed from storage and consumed, the date of the pit might be significantly later than the *mokkan*. We can only say, therefore, that the hole must have been filled in sometime *after* those dates.

In the summer of 1963, two years after the discovery of Pit SK219, another pit was found about 360 metres to the east. This pit, designated SK820 (4 metres square, 2.3 metres deep), yielded a large quantity of artifacts, including pottery, roof tiles, and wooden vessels, not to mention 1,843 *mokkan*. From the artifacts themselves and the way they had been buried, it was clear that this too was a rubbish pit used only for a very short time. The tablets in this pit provide us with excellent source materials for relating tablet dates and pit dates in general. The 67 datable tablets ranged over the 30-year period from 718 to 747 (fig. 37). The dates were not, however, evenly distributed over this span. Twenty tablets dated from between 718 and 732, and all were labels for tax shipments of silk floss or salt. By

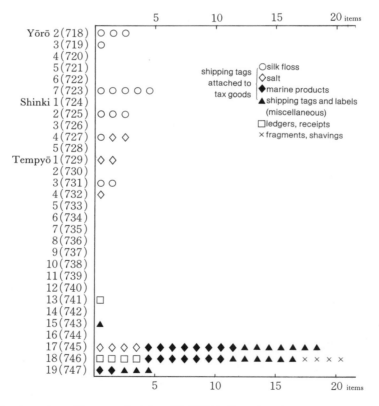

**37** A dated wooden tablet unearthed from Pit SK820. From just this one rubbish pit, 1,843 *mokkan* were unearthed; 67 were inscribed with reign dates, extending over a 30-year period. This rubbish pit was filled in 747 or slightly thereafter.

contrast, 45 tablet dates were concentrated within the three years from 745 to 747. Among this later group were shipping tags for tax goods which were not suitable for lengthy storage, such as fish and shellfish, and also tablets which had served as ledgers, receipts, etc., for official business. Thus there was a major difference in content between the tablets from the early years and those from the last three years. We can perhaps conclude that the earlier dated shipping tags for salt and silk floss were kept along with the goods in storage over a long period of time and were finally consumed during the years indicated on the concentrated group of dated tablets, that is, the late 740s. These shipping tags were then thrown away, together with those from the perishable foodstuffs and the unneeded office records. If, however, this pit had not contained any of the later dated tablets, and we had encountered only the tags for the earlier silk floss and salt shipments, we might have been tempted into positing a quite erroneous date for the filling of the pit.

What about the case of the earlier Pit SK219? In the context of the present discussion, the following tablet takes on significance. Catalogued as Nara Palace *mokkan* No. 1, it falls into the category which we usually refer to as 'temple request' tablet (fig. 38). It reads:

—*front:* A temple request for: 1 *to* of red beans and 15 *shō* of soy sauce, Ōyuka-dokoro, vinegar, bean paste, etc.
—*back:* The above-mentioned four types of goods, [delivered to] Tsukuba-no-Myōbu's office, the sixth day of the third month

(A *shō* was about 0.7 litres; 10 *shō* constituted 1 *to*.) This tablet, 25.9 centimetres long, was a request from a certain temple for beans, soy sauce, vinegar, bean paste,

**38** *(left)*
'Temple request' *mokkan* from Pit SK219. This tablet, dated the sixth day of the third month of 763 or 764, is a requisition for food by a temple at which the retired empress was lodging.

**39** *(right)*
'Soybean' *mokkan* from Pit SK219. Even the shavings from tablet surfaces may yield fascinating information. The going price of soybeans is revealed in this inscription.

and so forth for use in Tsukuba-no-Myōbu's office. Unfortunately, we know only the day and month, not the year of the request. The meaning of 'Ōyuka-dokoro' is also unclear.

Tsukuba-no-Myōbu, who appears in the *Shoku-Nihongi* chronicle in entries between 761 and 776, was the daughter of a prosperous and influential local family of Tsukuba County in the province of Hitachi (modern Ibaragi Prefecture). She was originally sent to Nara to serve in the status known as *uneme*. *Uneme* were young women selected from the provinces to serve as attendants to the emperor, pre-paring meals and carrying out various other similar chores. At the beginning of the eighth century, there were at the most between 100 and 200 *uneme* at court, since they were being sent to the capital at the rate of one young woman per every three counties. But by the middle of the century the figure was specified as one *uneme* per county. If these specifications were in fact carried out, there must have been over 500 *uneme* at court. Many of these young women were called by the name of their home county. A very few of them eventually managed to rise to the status of *myōbu* (Lower Fifth Rank) and thus come to rank on a par with the court ladies of noble origins.

Throughout her years at the palace, Tsukuba-no-Myōbu was in the service of Empress Kōken (who later became Empress Shōtoku). Since she was promoted from *uneme* to *myōbu* in 761, it is certain that the wooden tablet quoted above dates from no earlier than 761. During this time, she was supervising the preparation of the empress's meals, but the tablet makes it clear that her workplace was in a temple—which means that Empress Kōken must also have been living in a temple at the time.

By 761, Kōken had already retired and put Junnin on the throne. In the tenth month of 761, Junnin and the retired empress moved to Hora Palace in Ōmi Prov-ince while repairs were carried out at Nara; they remained there until the fifth month of 762. By that time a falling-out had occurred between the emperor and the retired empress as to who was to preside over the affairs of state, so when they returned to Nara, the retired empress moved into Hokkeji, the temple just east of the palace grounds. In the tenth month of 764 the retired empress deposed Junnin and took power under the name Shōtoku; she certainly must have returned to reside in the palace at that time. Thus Kōken would have lived in a temple for at most two years and five months. Therefore, the date 'sixth day of the third month' would have fallen in either 763 or 764. (Incidentally, Tsukuba-no-Myōbu eventu-ally returned to her home as *kuni-no-miyatsuko*—the highest rank in the district's religious hierarchy. This was an unprecedented honour for a woman.)

When the above-mentioned goods, which had been requested on the sixth day of the third month of 763 or 764, were finally received, the tablet was no longer need-ed and could have been thrown away immediately. It would then be reasonable to assume that trash pit SK219 was filled in not long after the delivery date. There is another piece of evidence which offers additional support for this conclusion. It is a shaving bearing the notation 'soybeans, 2 *shō*, price 22 *mon*' (fig. 39) and thus in-dicating that the price of 1 *shō* of soybeans came to 11 *mon* during those times.*
One *shō* was about 0.7 litres. According to records found in the Shōsōin, a treasure storehouse built in the eighth century and belonging to Tōdaiji temple, the price of

1 *shō* of soybeans was 5 *mon* in 748, 8 *mon* in the third month of 763, then jumped to 18 *mon* by the third month of 764 and to 20 *mon* by the twelfth month of that same year. The price must have stood at 11 *mon* sometime between the third month of 763 and that of 764. This fits well with our dating of the 'temple request' tablet found in the same pit.

Incidentally, prices in general rose throughout the eighth century. For example, the price of 100 *shō* of rice stood at around 66 *mon* in 711, at 2.5 times this value in 737, at 7.5 times this value in 751, and by 762 had increased more than 10 times to 700 *mon*. Two years later in 764, it reached 1,000 *mon* and the next year leapt to 2,000 *mon!* The price seems to have peaked around the year 770. In 762, a coolie's daily wages were about 10 *mon*. The phenomenal rise in prices was apparently due to a series of epidemics and disastrous harvests during the early 760s, as well as to mistaken government monetary policy.

As a result of the chain of reasoning outlined above, the date of filling in Pit SK219 can be put confidently at around 763 or 764. Shipping tags dug up from the same pit were dated 761 and 762, so in this case at least we find close agreement between the dates on the shipping tags and the date of filling in the pit.

Now let us take up the question of where the temple's request was taken to fill the order for foodstuffs. There are two candidates, both belonging to the Department of Palace Affairs: the Great Catering Office and the Inner Catering Bureau. The latter was charged chiefly with preparing meals for the emperor. The former, besides overseeing the Inner Catering Bureau, was responsible for all other catering within the palace, for receiving and storing foodstuffs remitted as taxes from the countryside, and for preparing processed foods such as soy sauce, bean paste, dried fruits, and rice cakes. Thus it would have been more appropriate for this particular temple request to be presented to the Great Catering Office. This leads to the further hypothesis that the area around Pit SK219 was probably occupied by that office at the time the order was placed, in 763 or 764.

## *Mokkan:* A rich source of information

There were many embedded-pillar buildings around Pit SK219 (fig. 40). Postholes from three of the buildings overlapped each other and the pit itself. Since the three buildings could not have stood on the same spot simultaneously, it can be assumed

---

*A very small number of coins manufactured in China have been recovered from Yayoi period sites in Japan; they were probably treated as mere curiosities at the time. The oldest extant coins actually minted in Japan are of silver and date from the later seventh century, but their circulation seems to have been quite limited. Large-scale manufacture and use of currency began in 708 with the minting of silver and copper coins. Two further mintings took place during the Nara period in 760 and 765; in 760, gold coins were issued as well. The vast majority of coins throughout the period were copper. The silver coins of 708 were equivalent to four copper coins, but hoarding of silver coins ensued, so they were taken out of circulation the year after their issue. For the minting of 760, copper coins were worth 1 *mon*, silver coins 10 *mon*, and gold coins 100 *mon*. In 765, the second Nara period minting, only copper coins were issued. On that occasion, the currency denomination changed, so that 1 *mon* in the new coinage was equivalent to 10 *mon* in the old coinage. The silver coins of the seventh century were irregular in shape (although roughly circular) but of uniform weight. The coins of 708 and later followed the Chinese model exactly: accurately circular, with a square hole in the centre and four Chinese characters surrounding the hole (see pl. 16).

that they were built at different times. Furthermore, since it is impossible to dig a pit where a pillar is standing, the pit and the pillars could not have coexisted. One of the three buildings, designated by the feature number SB205, should have had a centre pillar of its northern wall right where Pit SK219 lies—but there is no sign of the expected posthole.* Traces of the posthole, therefore, must have been eradicated when the pit was dug. Accordingly, Building SB205 must have been older than Pit SK219. Let us express this through the use of an arrow sign where → indicates 'older than': SB205 → SK219. Postholes from the other two buildings, SB209 and SB211—both overlapping Building SB205 from the north—were found visible on the surface of the dirt which filled Pit SK219; thus the postholes of those two buildings must have been dug after the pit was filled in. In other words, SK219→SB209/SB211. There were also separate locations where postholes from SB209 and SB211 overlapped each other. A careful examination of these cases reveals that the square edges of the postholes of SB211 are completely intact, while those of SB209 have been partially destroyed by the postholes of SB211. Thus SB209→SB211. Putting the chronology of the site all together, we can conclude: SB205→SK219→SB209→SB211.

Building SB209 had eight pillars on its longer, north-south dimension and three pillars across. Calculating 29.6 centimetres to the *shaku*, the pillar spacing is a consistent 10 *shaku*. To the south and east of SB209 were two more buildings of absolutely identical scale and structure. These were designated SB206 and SB213. If we run an imaginary line through the dead centres of the pillars of the north-south dimension of SB209 and extend it to the south, we find that pillars on the longer side of SB206 fall directly on that line. SB213 to the east differs from these two in that its longer dimension runs east-west, but otherwise it is identical in scale and structure. The northern pillar line of SB213 also runs through the short northern side of SB209. Measuring from the nearest edges, SB209 is precisely 20 *shaku* north of SB206 and exactly 40 *shaku* west of SB213. Since the pillars of these three buildings can all be situated on a common grid demarcated in units of 10 *shaku*, there is no doubt that they were designed and erected according to the same plan. One can assume that their eaves and ridgepoles would have lined up and that even the height of their roofs would have been identical. A few other buildings including SB201 were also part of this construction plan.

In such ways can we determine the relative age of archaeological features or postulate their coexistence. Examining the neighbourhood of the Great Catering Office in this light, we find that there were three major phases of building in the area during the Nara period. If major repairs and renovations are included, we can discern a total of five significant phases of construction, referred to here as Phases I.1, I.2, II.1, II.2, and III. (Interestingly, it seems that the land and buildings of the Great Catering Office were at first treated as two distinct spatial units, later being divided into four and finally six units. This fissioning process would seem to reflect an increasing complexity of the Office's administrative structure.) Of the

---

*Features excavated at Nara Palace and Capital are given reference numbers, sequential within each category of feature and starting with the first excavation. The category is indicated by a two-letter prefix: SK for pits; SB for buildings; SA for fences, walls, and other such boundary markers; SD for ditches; SE for wells; and so forth. The total number of features has already passed 20,000.

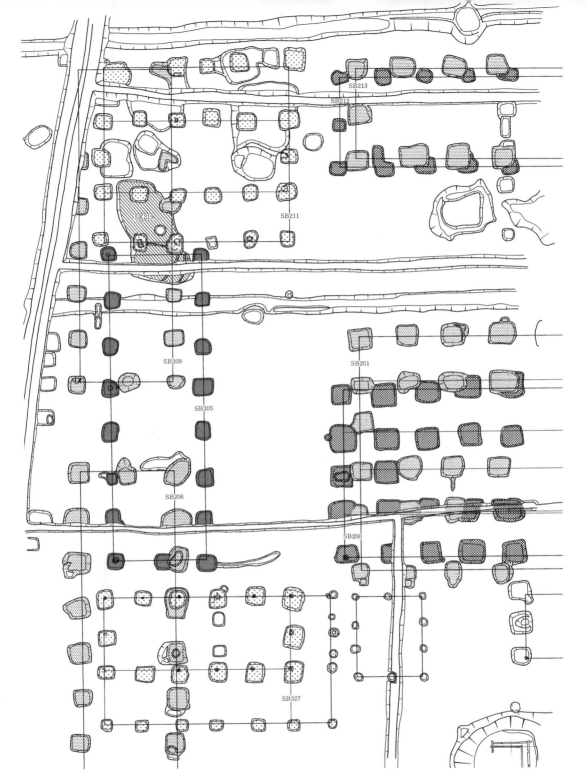

**40** The overlapping patterns of pillared buildings near Pit SK219. The dates of the buildings can be estimated from the relationships of the overlapping rubbish pit, filled in 763–64, and the postholes.

buildings which overlapped Pit SK219, SB205 belongs to Phase I.2; SB209 and the other buildings included in the same building plan fall into Phase II.1; and SB211 dates from Phase III.

All we have done thus far is determine the historical succession—the *relative dating*—of the various structures. We still have to find out exactly *when* each building was erected, that is, we need to clarify their *absolute dating*. At this point it is important to try to fix the date at which Pit SK219 was filled in. SK219 falls between Phases I.2 and II.1; thus I.2 ends before 763–64 and II.1 begins after.

The above examples of methods of dating relied on clues such as mutual relationships between building column postholes, overlapping relationships between postholes and pits, and the relative positioning of two or more buildings. In fact, any feature remaining in the ground—ditches, base stones, podia for gates or buildings—can be investigated using the same methodology, thus leading to postulations concerning relative and absolute dating. There are yet other ways of determining relative dating, or what archaeologists like to call 'establishing a chronology'. One of the most important is *stratigraphy*, on the assumption that younger layers of earth (and the artifacts and features they contain) lie above the older layers. One can also carry out stylistic comparisons of excavated artifacts. It is also possible to study the quality and contents of the earth filling particular features. For example, we may posit the simultaneity of two postholes if they contain similar traces of ash or charred wood from the destruction of a building by fire. The synthesis of all such lines of evidence helps to establish a chronology of features. The methods of determining relative dating, that is, of constructing a chronology, are in principle identical whether one is working with Nara Palace or with the prehistoric periods.

There is, however, one major difference between working with the prehistoric periods and working with remains at Nara Palace. For Nara, we have access to historical written documents which often allow us to infer the absolute dating of features. That is to say, with the Nara period we are in the realm of what is called historical archaeology. For example, when we find a reference in the *Shoku Nihongi* chronicle to an incident of building or repair work at Nara Palace, it is no easy matter to sort out from among several overlapping features the one to which the chronicle refers. Furthermore, there is no guarantee that all incidents of construction work have been recorded in the documentary evidence. *Mokkan* are different. Although even with these tablets we are often forced to rely on assumptions and hypotheses, in many cases they make it possible to fix directly and in precise detail the absolute dates of features and of their artifacts. It is no exaggeration to say that research methods at Nara Palace have undergone a revolution since the discovery of the first *mokkan*. It is chiefly because of the 'temple request' tablet found in Pit SK219 that the region surrounding the pit has been designated as the probable location during at least one length of time of the Great Catering Office of the Department of Palace Affairs.

By contrast, incidentally, absolute dating for Yayoi period (3rd century B.C.–A.D. 3rd century) sites, insofar as it is possible, rests principally on datable artifacts manufactured in China and imported into Japan. Many Chinese bronze mirrors from the end of the Western Han period (206 B.C.–A.D. 24) have been found as grave-goods in association with Middle Yayoi jar burials in northern Kyūshū; it is this fact that allows us to assign to the Middle Yayoi period an absolute date of around the beginning of the Christian era. As we go back further in time from that point, it becomes progressively more difficult to find datable artifacts of this kind. We are therefore forced to turn to other less reliable methods, such as those derived from the natural sciences. For example, the claim that pottery was being made in the Japanese archipelago by 10000 B.C. is based solely on the results of radiocarbon dating, a method developed in the United States after the Second World War.

Another dating method derived from the natural sciences, which has recently gained great currency at Nabunken and elsewhere in Japan, is dendrochronology. As its name suggests, this method traces back through time the fluctuating patterns in the annual growth rings of trees. A standard pattern is first determined and then compared with patterns taken from yet undated trees and wooden artifacts. If the patterns match, the artifacts can be dated. The method was pioneered in the United States at the start of the century and soon spread to Europe. The width of the growth rings reflects climatic and other environmental conditions in the immediate area, so that all trees of a given type in the area should show a fairly similar pattern of ring thickness for a given span of years. By joining up the patterns of trees of overlapping date, it is possible to establish a continuous series covering a given span of time. If the date of even one of the trees is known, the whole series can be dated. (This is obviously easiest if the series extends up to the present, since living trees can be dated precisely.) In this case, when an undated piece of wood is found—say, a pillar or a wooden vessel from an archaeological site—its pattern of rings can be compared with the master series to determine its relative as well as its absolute age. If the outermost growth ring survives, then we can determine the exact point in the series at which the particular tree was felled.

Although learning of dendrochronology quite early, Japanese researchers quickly concluded that the method was not suitable for use in their country. This conclusion was based partly on the misconception that the method was only useful in areas of minimal climatic variation, such as Arizona where it was originally developed, and partly on a failure to understand the method correctly. It was only in 1979 that a Nabunken member had the opportunity to observe the method firsthand in Europe, especially at Hamburg University under Professor D. Eckstein, and began to consider its potential usefulness in Japan. After several years of trial and error, while Professor Eckstein himself was in Japan, dendrochronology finally became a viable methodology in 1985. As a result, researchers established a series for Japanese cypress extending from the present back to 317 B.C., and it is now being applied to the dating of sites, features, and artifacts recovered from Nara Palace and Nara Capital.

*Mokkan* are not only valuable as direct evidence for the dating and actual character of features. By reference to the date recorded on Nara Palace *mokkan* No. 1—the 'temple request' tablet—we were able to draw the inference that the retired Empress Kōken, having entered Hokkeji temple after her return from Hora Palace (Ōmi Province) in the fifth month of 762, must have remained in residence there at least until the third month of 763 or even until the third month of 764. Apart from this tablet, there is no other documentary evidence to tell us when she left Hokkeji. A small matter, perhaps, but it demonstrates the potential of *mokkan* to fill the gaps in the historical record.

Shipping tag (*nifuda*) *mokkan* have contributed to a better understanding of the intricacies involved in the ancient tax system. In the Nara period there were basically three kinds of taxes, *so*, *yō*, and *chō*. *So* was a land tax paid out of the rice harvested from fields allotted to citizens by the government. Calculations show that the rate was about 3 per cent. *Chō* and *yō* were head taxes levied according to the age and health of the payer. Originally, *chō* was a tax in kind, while *yō* was levied in the form of a specified period of labour. However, this corvée obligation could be avoided through a payment in kind. Both *chō* and *yō* substitutions were most commonly paid in textile products including linen cloth, silk, and thread, but *chō* was also paid in products specific to particular localities such as coastal and mining areas. While *so* was paid to the local authorities, in principle, payments of *chō* and *yō* included the cost of delivering the goods to Nara Capital. This represented a very heavy burden on taxpayers. Residents of each province also owed a miscellaneous corvée tax (*zōyō*) of sixty days per year to the provincial governor. There were many other taxes and service obligations—one of which was *nie*. The characters *nie* and *chō* often occur on shipping tag tablets found in Nara Palace.

*Nie* may be considered to have been a type of tax requiring the rendering of foodstuffs. However, there were no official laws specifying the payment of *nie*. Although there are passing references to the custom in the Engi Shiki collection of procedures, we would be virtually in the dark concerning the practice in the eighth century, were it not for *mokkan*, of which *nie* shipping tags make up a large portion. *Nie* marine products and other foodstuffs were intended for the emperor's table, so perhaps the absence of a specific law is only natural. After all, the emperor was in essence above or beyond the law: he made the laws, and the people obeyed them. Of the 1,843 tablets discovered in Pit SK820 (see above, pp. 70–71), 46 are shipping tags for *nie*. The first of these, discovered in 1963, carried the following inscription:

> —The *ama-be* of Mikawa Province, Hazu County, Shino Island, hereby furnish *nie* for the fifth month: 6 *kin* [unit of weight] of dried shark meat.

Shino is a small island between the Chita and Atsumi Peninsulas in modern Aichi Prefecture. The *ama-be*, a group of fisherfolk, affixed this *mokkan* to one of their regular *nie* tribute. Considering the honorific prefix used with character for *nie* (viz. *mi-nie*), one can well believe that this shipment was intended for the emperor's personal consumption. On other tablets the character *nie* is sometimes preceded by the character for 'great, grand' (viz. *ō-nie*), perhaps signifying a similar honorific appellation. Let us take one more example:

> —*front:* Bizen Province, jellyfish, special tribute *nie*, 2 *to* [unit of volume]
> —*back:* 25th day of the ninth month, the eighteenth year of Tempyō [746].

The phrase 'special tribute' is interesting, for it once again shows an awareness that a *nie* is no ordinary tax. It appears possible, however, that during the Nara period *nie* goods were not consumed by the emperor alone but also by officials of noble origin. The conditions under which the *nie mokkan* were unearthed tend to support this hypothesis. Incidentally, since dried jellyfish today is used only in Chinese cooking, it would be interesting to know how the ancient Japanese prepared it.

Since the first discovery of tablets referring to *nie* at Nara Palace, many similar tablets have been found at Fujiwara Palace. Since the late 1960s, these finds have led to rapid advances in research on the institution of *nie*. Discussion has ranged from questions concerning its very nature to those of the evolution of the institution over time. It is now held that originally there was little difference between *nie* and *chō* (taxes in kind), save that the former involved foodstuffs, the latter other materials. Moreover, no distinction was made between rendering them to the emperor and to the state. With the establishment and stabilization of the various state administrative institutions during the later seventh century, a distinction was at last drawn: between *nie* as special food furnished for the emperor, and *chō* as official tax payments to the state. At the same time, *chō* came to include foodstuffs as well. The change may have taken place around the time of moving the capital from Fujiwara to Nara. In any case, in tracing the process of establishment of the tripartite tax system of *so* (rice tax), *chō*, and *yō* (corvée tax), one important clue will be to elucidate the details of *nie*, a task for which we are virtually totally dependent on *mokkan*.

Among the wooden tablets recovered at Nara Palace, there is one group which has a distinctive shape. From the front or back they appear no different from the rest, but viewing them edgewise reveals a tiny hole bored through the upper part. These tablets share an interesting feature in terms of content as well. Consider the following example (fig. 41):

> —*front:* Lower Junior Initial Rank, Takaya-no-muraji Yakamaro (of the Right Capital, age 50); six-year evaluation, total work days 1,099. (Sixth year: Average)
> —*back:* Divination Bureau

Civil service appointments carried with them ranked status, a salary appropriate to the post, and a tax exemption. There were thirty ranks in all from Senior First Rank at the top to Lower Junior Initial Rank at the bottom. Takaya-no-muraji Yakamaro thus held the very lowest rank. He was fifty years old, hailed from the Right Capital (the western district of Nara Capital), and worked at the Divination Bureau, which was in charge of time-keeping, calendrics, divination, and so forth. His six-year work evaluation was based on 1,099 work days; in other words, he had spent an average of 181 days per year 'at the office'. In eighth-century Japan, only the officials of higher rank were allowed to appear for work every day. Lesser officials could work only a limited number of days on a sort of shift system. Yakamaro, holding the lowest rank, was obviously one of these alternating bureaucrats. Officials of the lower ranks could not survive on their government salaries alone, so they would supplement their incomes by farming on their off-days. Still, they must not let their agricultural activities interfere with their attendance at the office, for fear of receiving an unsatisfactory work evaluation. If they did not put in at least 140 days, they would not be subject to evaluation and possible promotion. With his average of 181 days per year, Yakamaro was at least

**41**
A wooden tablet used as a work evaluation form for a bureaucrat. Much in the manner of modern file cards, one *mokkan* was filled out for evaluating the work of each bureaucrat.

eligible for evaluation. For these lower-ranking alternating bureaucrats, the first chance at possible promotion came after six years of evaluations, and further chances came every six years after that. Higher-ranking officials were considered for promotion every fourth year. (In certain other cases, the period was eight or ten years.) According to this tablet, Yakamaro's six-year rating was 'Average'. With such an evaluation, how far might he have been promoted? The tablet is silent on this point. Even with a 'Superior' rating, one could hope to advance perhaps three ranks at best. In addition to these regular opportunities for promotion and salary increases, it was also possible to receive a special promotion. One example, recorded on another tablet, is the two-rank advancement for a man who had served as an envoy to Bohai (a country in northeastern China during the eighth and tenth centuries).

A number of these tablets bearing the results of work evaluations have been found. Each referred to a single person, giving his rank, name, age, birthplace, and evaluation rating for the previous years. More than 80 per cent of the ratings were Superior; the rest were Average. There are no examples of an Inferior rating, suggesting perhaps that the evaluation process had become somewhat of a formality. It is interesting to note, however, that nearly half of these tablets bore no rating at all, but only the notation 'not evaluated', due to the fact that the candidate had failed to work the minimum number of days required.

All of these work-evaluation tablets had a hole edge to edge through their upper end. Presumably the tablets could then be joined by a length of string, allowing them to be grouped by rating, and then perhaps re-arranged by civil service rank. Each string of tablets would then be copied by clerks onto paper in order to prepare the final forms. The tablets were the equivalent of our modern-day filing card systems. This system, however efficient it may have been, appears to have died out by the beginning of the medieval period.

Nearly all of these work-evaluation tablets were recovered in 1966 from a single location, a rain gutter lying just inside the eastern end of the palace's south Great Wall. In all, nearly 10,000 such tablets were found there. There were also many shavings among them. The same tablet could be used for the same individual for each evaluation and promotion, simply by shaving off the old notation. In that sense, we might say, *mokkan* were even better suited to this particular use than paper file cards would have been. Matters involving personnel and work evaluation were the province of the Ministry of Ceremonies. Presumably, then, this ministry was located not far from the rain gutter in which the tablets were found.

There is no end to the historical questions to whose solution *mokkan* can contribute. The story could fill several books—in fact, it already has.


During the thirty years since the first *mokkan* appeared from Pit SK219 at Nara Palace, further tablets have been found not only at sites in other ancient capitals—Fujiwara, Nagaoka, and Heian—but also at ancient temples and administrative centres scattered throughout Japan. In all, nearly four hundred sites have produced a total of 150,000 tablets. Among them some 33,000 have been found at the Nara Palace site. These days, an excavator at any site from the historical era is almost certainly waiting expectantly for some *mokkan* to surface, since the tablets can reveal so much information about the site. Furthermore, because they are actually found *in situ*, the interpretation of the evidence provided by *mokkan* is slightly different in nature from that for other written historical documents. Therefore, it has now become necessary to carry out research on the tablets in an interdisciplinary way, eliciting the help not only of historiographical experts but also of archaeologists and related scientists. One response to this need was the formation in 1978 of the Japanese Society for the Study of Wooden Documents. The Society holds research seminars and has begun publication of a society journal, half of which is devoted to reporting news of the previous year's finds, while the remaining pages are given over to research papers. It is now almost certain that the Japanese tablets developed from the Chinese practice as a means of facilitating the adoption and implementation of a Chinese-style legal system. Thus comparative research on tablets from the two countries is essential. Research is also gradually extending to such spheres as the political, social, economic, religious, and philological significance of the tablets.

Now having come upon 150,000 new historical documents, of a type whose existence was not known only thirty years ago, we must make the most of what they have to tell us. For this purpose, a computer data base for *mokkan* has been set up at Nabunken, as part of the Buried Cultural Properties Information Retrieval System. This data base contains not only the original inscription (in Chinese characters), but also the artifact serial number, the site and feature where recovered, form classification, dimensions, type of wood, method of cutting, extent of damage, classification of content, date of excavation, photograph number, pertinent bibliographical references, and separate entries for any personal or place names and any dates mentioned in the inscription. In all, there are sixteen categories of data plus the original text for each tablet. If one is interested in, for example, all tablets referring to tribute of the *nie* type, or all the shavings, one has only to punch in the key word to receive an instantaneous listing of all relevant tablets, their original text, and sixteen categories of information. Expectations for this computer resource are great, and there have even been requests from researchers abroad wishing to use the data base.

## The science of *mokkan* preservation

The bottom of Pit SK219, where the first *mokkan* was found, lies about 1 metre beneath the level of the present paddy surface, and was constantly inundated with ground water. Apart from pottery and roof tiles, there was a varied range of organic material in the pit. In addition to the wooden tablets, there were seeds, leaves, twigs, bark, charcoal, and other fragments of charred wood. It was not only because of the depth at which they lay, safe from the plough and other disturbances, that these organic items survived: it was also because they were constantly wet, the ground water keeping them in an airtight environment, protected from the invasion of decay-causing bacteria. These items were not however sheltered from all change. The cellulose and various resinous components which constitute the major part of wood were leached away to less than a tenth of the proportion which they occupy in living wood, and their place was taken by the surrounding water. Thus the aqueous component of these items was much greater than in their lifetimes —often as much as ten times greater by weight. When such a waterlogged object is removed from the ground, it may look structurally healthy from the outside, but as water loss and rapid dessication ensue, it is almost certain to shrink, crack, or otherwise lose its original shape. Sometimes it may even fall to pieces. The job of preventing this falls to the specialists known as conservators. There are basically three weapons available to them in the battle to preserve waterlogged wooden artifacts: the PEG method, the freeze-drying method, and the alcohol-ether-dammar method.

PEG is an abbreviation for polyethylene glycol, a high polymer whose molecular weight may range anywhere from about 200 to 20,000; the useable range in preservation is from 300 to 6,000. When the molecular weight is high, the polymer is white and waxy; at lower values, it takes the form of a sticky liquid. Polyethylene glycol is a frequent component of commercial skin treatment products. The form most widely used in the preservation of waterlogged wood is PEG-4000, with a mean molecular weight of 3,700. Although a solid at normal temperatures, it melts at 55°C and also dissolves in water. For conserving excavated waterlogged wooden objects, a 20 per cent solution of PEG-4000 in water is maintained in a tank at a constant 60°C, and the artifacts are immediately plunged into it. As the water contained in the artifact begins to merge with the PEG solution, the concentration of PEG in the tank is gradually increased until at last it stands at 98 to 100 per cent. The water originally trapped in the artifact will eventually be totally replaced by PEG—but it takes some time. A pillar root with a diameter of 30 centimetres will need to remain submerged for about one year. When the object is finally removed and exposed to normal temperatures, the PEG hardens in place and the shape of the object is safely preserved. Its weight, however, will be approximately 1.2 times the weight prior to treatment.

The freeze-drying method is basically identical with the process used for instant coffee and other dried foods. In dealing with foodstuffs, the water in the item is first frozen solid and then induced to sublimate in a vacuum: the ice is transformed directly into water vapour without passing through a liquid stage. In the case of wooden artifacts, the process is slightly more complex than described above: first the water is replaced by the organic solvent tert-butanol, with PEG as a pre-treatment; it is this solvent that is frozen and then sublimated. This reduces both the drying time and the risk of damage. Tert-butanol freezes at $-40°C$; as the temperature is raised to $+30°C$ at an atmospheric pressure of 1/7000, it sublimates rapidly. An object the size of a matchbox will dry in about ten hours. If some PEG is put into solution with the tert-butanol in advance, it will remain behind to strengthen the wood as in the normal PEG method. If carried out skilfully, this method can prevent shrinkage or other damage to the object.

In the alcohol-ether-dammar method, the water in the artifact is first replaced by alcohol. Meanwhile, various natural resins such as dammar resin, beeswax, and rosin are dissolved in ether. When the alcohol-drenched object is placed in this solution, the alcohol dissolves in the ether and the resinous solution impregnates the wood. Upon drying, the ether evaporates and the resins remain in place. However, as it is difficult to effect the absorption of large quantities of resin, there is some danger of shrinkage or distortion. Thus, this method is only suitable for the preservation of relatively thin objects.

Each of these three methods has its particular strengths and weaknesses. The choice will depend on the nature of the artifact: the type of wood, the shape, the condition of preservation, etc. At present, it is the freeze-drying method that is most useful for *mokkan*.

The adoption and full operationalization of these methods of wood preservation in Japan came several years after the first discoveries of wooden tablets. Although some preliminary research and a few small-scale experiments were being conducted, advanced preservation methods were not yet regularly available. The first *mokkan* were sealed in gelatin to prevent desiccation, then stored under cool, humid, antiseptic conditions. The first specialist in these conservation techniques to be appointed at Nabunken, in 1969, was Sawada Masaaki, a graduate in conservation sciences from Tokyo National University of Fine Arts and Music.

## Ceramic research: *Haji* ware

The importance of *mokkan* in determining the date and function of archaeological features is now abundantly clear. The identification of the Great Catering Office, the *Sake*-making Bureau, and the Ministry of Ceremonies all rest on the evidence of the tablets. But *mokkan* are not the only artifacts to bear writing. Some ceramics with inscriptions in China ink have provided evidence similar to that of the tablets. We have already referred to the value of these 'ink-inscribed ceramics' in Chapter 2. There we mentioned a potsherd bearing the name of the Music Bureau, which was instrumental in leading to the inference that the western south gate of the Great Wall was named Wakainukai (see p. 34). The identification of the *Sake*-making Bureau was partly based on the excavation there of potsherds bearing references to *sake* (see p. 23).

The Nabunken Nara Palace Museum today stands just northeast of the site of the palace's middle west gate. From 1968 to 1970, before the museum was built, a series of excavations was conducted in the area: Excavations Nos. 47, 50–52, 59, 63, and 71. It was inferred from the traces of embedded pillar buildings and board fences that a single office compound had occupied a space some 100 metres east-west and 250 metres north-south (fig. 42). The compound had an interesting feature: despite evidence of frequent construction activity at the site throughout the eighth century, there had apparently never been a building in the centre of the compound. As for the various pillared buildings surrounding this vacant plaza, they were all three to five pillars wide on their shorter sides, but on their longer sides they measured from 15 to 22 pillars wide. In both building size and layout, this office compound was unique within the palace. One of the Nabunken researchers, who had formerly worked with horses in the old Imperial Japanese Army, felt sure that the buildings had been stables. In that case, the plaza in the middle could have been a riding ground. But where was the proof? On the featural evidence alone, this had to remain a hypothesis.

At this point, three sherds from ink-inscribed pottery vessels came to the rescue. The sherds, excavated from this compound, bore the words 'Inner Stables' and 'Royal Mews'. The Bureau of Inner Stables was established in 765, during a reorganization of the military officers serving close to the emperor. The Bureau of Royal Mews is known to have existed by 781, although its date of establishment is uncertain. True to their names, both of these bureaux dealt with the maintenance of horses. According to the administrative system of the early eighth century, matters pertaining to horses should have been the province of the Left and Right Equestrian Bureaux, but the system apparently changed during the course of the century. Oddly enough, by the year 808 at Heian Palace, the Bureau of Inner Stables and Bureau of Royal Mews had vanished and the two Equestrian Bureaux had reappeared. At any rate, the ink-inscribed pottery vessels confirmed the old soldier's instincts: these were indeed stables. It should be remembered that at Heian Palace the Equestrian Bureaux also stood just inside the west wall of the palace grounds and that excavations at the Fujiwara Palace site revealed traces of a group of long buildings, oriented north-south, just inside the western palace wall.

The vessel bearing the words 'Royal Mews' (fig. 43) was discovered in an ancient well, safely sealed in the subsurface water. If wooden tablets had been in this well, they too would have been protected by the moisture. The conditions which help to preserve wooden artifacts are equally important for ceramics. The 'Royal Mews' vessel was in strikingly good condition. Of the ceramic vessels excavated at the Nara Palace site, the vast majority are of the type known as *haji* ware; *sue* ware constitutes another 20 to 30 per cent; and there is a tiny quantity of surface-glazed pottery. *Haji* ware is a continuation of a ceramic tradition from the Yayoi period. Made without a wheel and fired without a kiln, it is a relatively low-fired, porous earthenware. Firing temperatures were in the range of 600 to 800°C. *Sue* ware is made on a wheel and fired in kilns which were introduced from the Korean Peninsula during the fifth century. It is fired at around 1250°C and is usually a hard, blue-grey stoneware. The few glazed wares available to us reflect the glazing technology imported from Tang China. *Sue* vessels, being relatively hard, may survive with little deterioration, even when they are not particularly well insulated from surface disturbance. The *haji* and glazed wares, however, may weaken and, in extreme cases, turn brown and crumble to pieces if they occur too near the surface. For this reason, the same kind of conditions that allowed the first *mokkan* to survive so well in Pit SK219 would also be favourable to the preservation of *haji* and glazed wares.

Ceramic research has two principal aims. One is to use ceramic objects as clues in dating the sites and features from which they were excavated. For this, it is necessary to clarify the relative and absolute dates of the ceramics themselves. Among the artifacts which the archaeologist deals with, pottery is the most universally present in sites; furthermore, the clay from which it is made can assume almost any shape and carry a wide range of decorations. Because ceramics are so

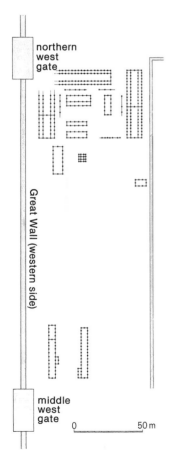

**42**
Layout of the Equestrian Bureau. Long rectangular buildings and a central open area were features suited to the Equestrian Bureau.

**43**
A vessel inscribed 'Royal Mews'. It is assumed that the Bureau of Royal Mews was located near the spot where this vessel was recovered.

rich in their variety of shape and decoration, their stylistic peculiarities are useful as criteria for distinguishing regions or eras of manufacture. Thus they are extremely valuable to the archaeologist. For example, the ceramic assemblage found in Pit SK219 must date from no later than 763–74. If stylistically similar pottery is found in an otherwise undated feature, it will be possible to infer information about the date of that feature as well.

The second major aim of ceramic research is to shed light on such matters as the system of ceramic production, the processes of change in technique, and the social history of the population which used the pottery. As a means to this end, it is desirable to reconstruct with as much certainty as possible, through minute scrutiny of the pottery, both the exact techniques of manufacture and the original function of each vessel. To achieve this second aim, it is important to be able to determine the period and place of manufacture. When a new item of pottery is found, the archaeologist's first concern is therefore to classify it typologically and to determine its date.

When pottery began to come out of Pit SK219, items worth studying in terms of what was already known about eighth-century ceramics were pitifully few. The total corpus of available evidence consisted of a group of vessels from a large ditch in the northeast corner of Nara Palace, excavated in 1928 and 1932; a few items found in a well beneath Hōryūji temple in 1934; and a large number of ceramics excavated in 1957 from Funahashi, a village site which lay in the bed of the Yamato River in Kashihara City, Osaka Prefecture. After much study, it became clear that the Funahashi pottery comprised two large groups, representing the first and second halves of the eighth century. At the Nara Palace site, investigators were eager to refine this rough chronology, and it became a major theme of their research.

Almost the entire yield of ceramics from the typical dig consists of dirt-caked sherds. In extracting useful information from such fragments, the first step is to wash off the dirt with water and with a brush if necessary. The brush must be wielded gently, in case the sherd bears ink writing. Rough brushwork may also damage the surface, hindering subsequent examination of the finer details of manufacture. After this bath, and a good drying off, the sherds are laid out and the work of reassembling the pottery begins. This process resembles a three-dimensional jigsaw puzzle—except that some of the pieces are almost certain to be missing.

As with a jigsaw puzzle, the trick in reassembling a pot is to study each piece carefully and fix its characteristics firmly in mind. It also helps to be able to develop an intuitive sense of where a given piece might lie in a complete pot. When a few thousand sherds have been filed in one's head in this way, the work of reconstruction proceeds smoothly. Put differently, this work involves a process of grasping the characteristics of a pot as it is pieced together. Work on the pottery from Pit SK219 led gradually to the development of an image of the ceramics of the years around 763–64.

As reassembling progresses, the date and place of excavation is recorded on each piece in tiny characters of ink, unobtrusively but clearly, since an artifact of unknown provenance loses much of its value as a resource.

During the reassembling process, the researchers make scale drawings, either of assembled pots or of individual sherds. The procedure with the items from Pit

SK219 was typical: an item was selected which epitomized the researchers' emerging image of the ceramics of 763–64. Each pot is laid on graph paper and drawn both in profile and in cross-section. If a 1:1-scale drawing is not feasible, an enlarged or reduced drawing can be made. Sometimes a bird's-eye view is also made. Once these drawings have been finished, any observations about the item are recorded on them. As with the reassembling process, the making of scale drawings is a good opportunity for the archaeologist to make detailed observations about the artifact. The making of scale drawings may bring out new elements unnoticed at the stage of reassembling. Tiny marks noted on the surface, or slight irregularities in shape, are almost certainly the results of the manufacturing process or else of daily use, and they can offer many clues to the secrets of the pot's past. Such deformities are revealed only through careful measurement. The process of measuring is not merely an aid to making scale drawings: it is also one means for the researcher to internalize the details of the artifact, as well as to concretize the images and to document the perceptions of the pottery that emerge during the stages of reassembly and drawing. Accordingly, it is only natural for two different observers to produce somewhat different scale drawings.

Once the scale drawings are completed, the researcher is basically finished with direct research on the physical artifact itself. Another task involving actual artifacts is carried out as reassemblage progresses. Using the partially or wholly reassembled items, as well as the other leftover sherds, the researcher groups together all the fragments that belong to each single ceramic object. Each object is classified morphologically, and a running count of the different shape-types is kept.

In Europe and North America, the work of reassemblage and drawing is usually performed by specialists in this field. In Japan, virtually all archaeologists are able (and in principle expected) to do these tasks themselves. Japanese archaeologists believe that these stages in the processing of ceramics—indeed, of all excavated objects—provide an important opportunity to examine these objects closely, to gain 'hands-on' familiarity with the products of the past. Leaving such tasks to others would mean that they would lose this opportunity. For this reason, Japanese archaeologists devote a good deal of time to these jobs.

The results of reassemblage suggest that the several thousand sherds recovered from Pit SK219 represent a total of 333 items of *haji* ware and 66 of *sue*—a ratio of five to one. In other excavations at Nara Palace, *sue* has consistently occurred in about this percentage or even less. However, at the Funahashi site in Osaka, the ratio of *haji* vessels to *sue* vessels was only three to two. If the proportion of *haji* at Nara Palace is unusually high, there must be a reason.

Over 90 per cent of the *haji* ware in Pit SK219 was tableware belonging to the three categories called by archaeologists *tsuki*, *wan*, and *sara* (figs. 44, 48). Since these types do not correspond well to English concepts such as 'cup' or 'bowl', we shall use the Japanese designations. There is only one type of *tsuki*, but both *wan* and *sara* come in two sizes, small and large. Each of these five types is quite consistent in size. Nara Palace was the scene of frequent banquets and other occasions involving great numbers of diners, so we would expect there to have been a large matched set of tableware. For the same reason, perhaps, there is a relative scarcity of *haji* storage jars and cooking pots or kettles (fig. 45). *Haji* jars are mostly

**44** *Haji* serving vessels. There were five types of *haji* tableware; the *haji* pedestaled plate in the background was doubtless also used in serving food.

**45** *Haji* kettles. During the Nara period, earthenware kettles were commonly used for cooking.

quite small, not intended for large-scale storage. In Pit SK219, these jars and cooking vessels constituted about 10 per cent of the assemblage; at Funahashi, by contrast, over half of the *haji* ware belonged to these categories. No doubt the chefs at Nara Palace used iron cooking pots and kettles for the typical large-scale palace meals, having little need for the smaller *haji* cooking ware. The ceramics found at the palace differ little in shape and quality from the everyday pottery recovered from village sites such as Funahashi; it is rather the relative proportions of the different types that reflect the special nature of Nara Palace. Indeed, not only at Pit SK219 but also at other locations at the palace, *haji* tableware was the most prevalent, while *haji* jars, cooking pots, and kettles were scarce, thus indicating one more characteristic feature in our developing image of life in Japan's ancient capitals. The special significance of ceramic research at the Nara Palace site became apparent as the contents of Pit SK219 were studied.

*Haji* tableware was abundant, cooking ware was scarce. This characteristic of Nara Palace stands out clearly, in comparison not only with the village site of Funahashi in Osaka Prefecture, but even with other locations within Nara Capital itself. An example is the excavation along the final route of the Nara Bypass, introduced in Chapter 1. Of the *haji* ware in a ditch from the early eighth century, almost 30 per cent were cooking pots and kettles. Clearly there was a great difference between the everyday cooking at the residences of the nobles and officials of Nara Capital and the banquets and other events within the palace itself.

A close examination of the *haji* tableware reveals that a very few examples have a leaf impression on the outside of the base (fig. 46). This is important for reconstructing the method of manufacture of the *haji* ware. There seems to have been a difference in manufacturing technique between vessels which were small enough to hold in the palm of the hand and those which were not. When making *sara, tsuki* and apparently larger *wan*, the potter would first prepare two oak leaves (*kashiwa;*

**46**
A leaf imprint on the base of a *haji* bowl. In making *haji* ware, the vessel was often set on a large leaf for shaping. The leaf was then moved like a turntable.

*Quercus dentata* [Thunb.]) or black alder leaves (*hannoki; Alnus japonica* [Thunb.] Steudel), placing them with their smooth sides together. Thus the veinous sides would be facing outwards. (The existence of the lower leaf is a hypothesis based on ethnographic examples.) Then a cord of well-kneaded clay would be pressed onto the centre of the upper leaf and gradually coiled outwards. On a few vessels it is even possible to see marks left by the fingers as they pressed the clay against the leaf. It is probable that a layer of clayey water separated the two leaves, acting as a lubricant. The veins of the upper leaf were embedded in the bottom of the vessel, providing traction; as the clay cord was coiled continuously outwards, the vessel and this upper leaf may have rotated on the lubricating layer. With this simple sort of rotating platform, the potter could coil the clay with minimal movement of body and hands. In this way the base of the vessel was prepared. Adding further cords, the potter then built up the sides to complete the rough form of the vessel.

The sides and the inside of the vessel were then smoothed with something like cloth or soft leather. In smoothing the sides, the thumb would rest on the inside surface and the other fingers on the outside, in a pincer movement, just as one might dry a wet bowl today. When a vessel is made on the potter's wheel, as with *sue* ware, the traces left by the smoothing process form bands parallel to the rim. The marks on the *haji* tableware, by contrast, tail diagonally upwards toward the rim as they come to an end (fig. 47 *top*). This is part of the evidence indicating that *haji* was not made on a wheel. Looking at a vessel and its 'tails' from above, it is obvious that the vast majority of *haji* items were smoothed in a clockwise direction. This is as expected, if we assume that most people were right-handed then as now. The pot-

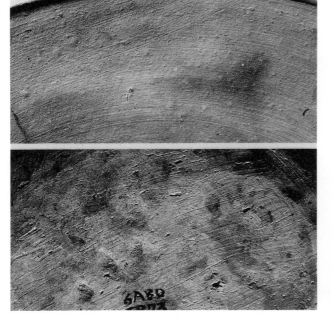

**47**
Manufacturing marks on *haji* ware. The surfaces of the vessels still carry the imprints of wiping with a piece of leather or cloth (*top*) and the facets from shaving (*bottom*). Such minute traces allow the reconstruction of the stages of manufacture and of changes in the ceramics over time.

ter's final task was to shave the base of the vessel to a suitable thickness from the outside with some sort of wooden tool (fig. 47 *bottom*); as a result, most of the vessels in Pit SK219 showed no vein marks. As mentioned, traces of veins were found only on the larger tableware and never on the smaller *wan*. The smaller vessels were apparently made in exactly the same way, except that the coil of clay was laid directly on the palm of the left hand. The above description shows how one can reconstruct virtually the entire manufacturing procedure up to this stage from minute clues on the surface of the pottery.

The vessel is then dried and fired. Traces of ancient firing sites have been discovered all over Japan in recent years. It seems that the standard procedure was to dig a rectangular or oval pit perhaps 3 to 4 metres long and 30 to 40 centimetres deep; the dried pottery and the requisite fuel were merely piled into the pit and the fuel was ignited. The type of covered or enclosed kiln used in the firing of *sue* ware and roof tiles was unknown in *haji* production.

Making *haji* ware in this fashion required the services of only one experienced artisan and an assistant. There was no need for a special potter's wheel as with *sue* ware, nor for a structually complex kiln. The simple *haji* trench was economical with respect to fuel, and it also avoided the problem of having to wait for firing until enough pottery was ready to fill the entire kiln. Documentary sources concerning *haji* production are scarce, but one source tells us that in at least one case a man and woman worked together as a team. The source can be interpreted as implying that the woman did the actual making of the vessel, while the man acted as an assistant and was in charge of digging the clay, kneading it, gathering firewood, securing straw for packing and other uses, and delivering the product to the capital. The woman and man produced 4,416 *haji* vessels in three months, delivered them to the relevant office, and received their wages. It has long been thought that *haji* ware and the pottery of the Yayoi period were made by women, while *sue* was made by men; but this document is the only concrete evidence concerning the production of *haji*.

If the diameter of the rim and the height of the *haji* ware from Pit SK219 are plotted on a graph, the points fall roughly into five groups (fig. 48). These correspond

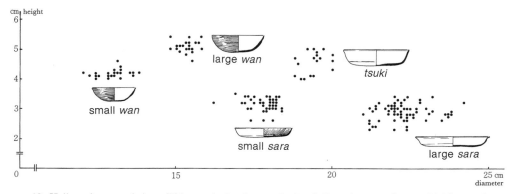

**48** *Haji* serving vessel sizes. This graph clearly reveals that *haji* serving vessels were highly standardized goods in 763–64.

to our intuitive typology of *tsuki*, large and small *sara*, and large and small *wan*. The consistency of dimensions within each type is what we would expect of a set of matched tableware intended for use at large-scale banquets and official meals. The existence of such a set also presupposes the presence by this time of a system of production able to supply these items. *Haji* ware is descended from the Yayoi pottery made in the farming villages. Originally, villagers with pottery skills produced earthenware for nearby communities in the agricultural off-season. (Among Yayoi pottery and the *haji* ware of the Tumulus period, the external bases of many pots show impressions of grains of rice. This fact leads to the hypothesis that these pots were made at a place and time at which rice grains could be found scattered around—namely, in farming villages during the post-harvest season. We have yet to see a single *haji* sherd from Nara Palace with such impressions.) In most cases, these farmer-potters would certainly have known the people who would be using their wares.

By the Nara period, the large-scale demand for *haji* ware of consistent sizes, to be used by distant, unknown consumers, had led to the emergence of a class of professional artisans who were paid in cash. This change in production relations constitutes a sharp and important transition in terms of the development of the crafts industry. These specialized artisans may well have found the centre of their livelihood shifting from agriculture to pottery.

Let us consider only the larger sizes of *haji* tableware from Pit SK219—those that were made with the two-leaf technique. Of a total of 148 vessels whose external finishing techniques could be ascertained, 7 per cent had not had their bases thinned, so that the leaf-vein marks remained (we shall call this method of surface treatment Technique A); 68 per cent had bases thinned with a wooden implement (Technique B); 22 per cent had been thinned not only on the bottom but on the entire external surface (Technique C); and the remaining 3 per cent had been carefully polished with a wooden implement so that the surface was smooth and shiny. Let us recall once more that these ceramics were buried in 763 or 764.

The excavation of Pit SK820 during the summer of 1963, in the northeastern palace grounds, produced 1,843 wooden tablets of which 67 bore era dates. From these dates we were able to infer that the pit had been filled in around the year 748. This pit also yielded over 600 items of *sue* and *haji* ware, as well as the beautiful three-colour glazed lid from a small jar (pl. 10). Of the *haji* tableware in this pit, an impressive 76 per cent was made by Technique A, with the leaf-vein marks still visible. Smooth-bottomed vessels (Technique B) constituted 20 per cent, and 4 per cent had been smoothed all over (Technique C). This is a clear and striking difference from the items of Pit SK219, which was filled in some fifteen years later.

Another excavation had already yielded a *haji* assemblage indicating a completely opposite trend from the assemblage in Pit SK820 in terms of finishing technique. These were the full set of wares from Well SE311, which lay within what were thought to be the precincts of the Great Catering Office in the north-central palace grounds. Ninety per cent of this assemblage had surfaces that had been given a completely smooth finish (Technique C), while the remaining 10 per cent had been made by a previously unknown Technique E. Techniques A and B were totally absent. Although this Well SE311 had existed since the eighth century, it was repaired and put into use again early in the next century. The wares in question came from the bottom of the newer well. A provisional dating of around 820 has been assigned to the filling-in of this well.

Through the observation of these three assemblages of *haji* tableware, we can discern a certain transformation process in the various methods of manufacture. In early eighth-century Yamato, Technique A was predominant. Soon Technique B appeared, and as it spread, a variant, Technique C, appeared. Towards the end of the century there was almost a total transition to Technique C, but from the early ninth century Technique C was gradually superseded by a new one, Technique E.

These changes in method of surface finishing were paralleled by changes in shape (fig. 49). The *tsuki* and *sara* made according to such techniques as A and B had flat bottoms and nearly vertical sides, with a clear, angular slope between bottom and sides. With the overall smoothing of Technique C, this angular slope became less distinct, but more striking is the fact that the sides now flared outwards at a much greater angle. If one wanted to smooth the entire outer surface, it was certainly easier if the sides were flared. The flaring mouth and the less distinct division between bottom and sides were both natural developments emerging from the adoption of Technique C. This is only a single example, but it is often the case that a change in shape may be correlated with the adoption of a new method of manufacture or the alteration of an old method.

It is through the careful tracing of such changes in shape or technique, and the relations between them, that archaeologists construct ceramic chronologies and

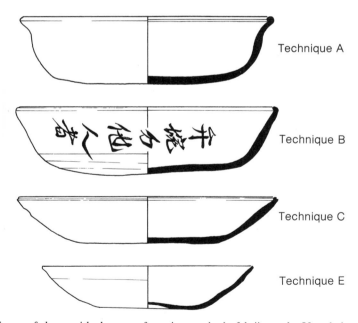

Technique A

Technique B

Technique C

Technique E

**49** Covariance of shape with the manufacturing method of *haji* vessels. Vessel shapes changed because of changes in production methods, and *vice versa*. In Japanese archaeological scale drawings of vessels, the left-hand side shows the vessel exterior, and the right-hand side shows the wall section and interior surface.

determine the relative ages of different items of pottery. If, for example, a pottery assemblage is discovered which contains about 50 per cent Technique C vessels and 20 per cent Technique B, then we can situate this assemblage in time somewhere between those of Pit SK219 and Well SE311, that is, somewhere between 763–64 and approximately 820. The ink-inscribed 'Royal Mews' vessel mentioned above (fig. 43) was a *haji tsuki*, finished by Technique C and with flaring sides; these and other details of its manufacture help us to date it provisionally to the very end of the Nara period.

The method of research is in principle the same for other artifacts besides ceramics, demanding careful observation of changes in shape, manufacture, and usage. Furthermore, the same approach is valid both for periods when we have written records available, such as the Nara period, and for the prehistoric era. In other words, observation always leads to hypotheses about the relative dates of such changes. The major difference between the prehistoric and historic periods is a simple but crucial one. In the latter case it is possible to determine absolute, calendar dates as well as relative ones. It is theoretically possible, for example, to investigate questions such as, How do ceramic traditions change in a period of fifty years? or a period of twenty-five years? With prehistoric artifacts, the answers to such questions are virtually inaccessible.

We have described ceramic research based on careful observation of minute details of the artifacts. In truth, to the unpractised eye it may be very hard to distinguish between categories of Nara pottery, since they all look very much alike. This is largely because the pottery of this period is almost totally lacking in decoration or surface designs, especially in comparison with the richly ornamented ceramics of the Jōmon (10000–300 B.C.) and Yayoi periods. The extreme simplicity of the Nara wares is presumably a reflection of a stress on the functional and practical at the expense of the aesthetic. This is not to say that decoration is totally absent. In the case of the *haji* tableware, from its first appearance in the seventh century until the early eighth century, the inner surfaces of almost all items carried many patterns of etched or gently polished lines (fig. 50). Designs were apparently rubbed into the clay with the blunt tip of a smooth, thin wooden stylus. The rubbed sections reflected light differently from the neighbouring rougher areas, creating a subdued yet beautiful decorative effect. The centre of the inner base was usually rubbed in a pattern of curlicues and might be surrounded by radial or scallop patterns of thinner lines. This type of internal decoration is called a 'hidden design' (although of course it was intended to be seen). An item with a hidden design on the inside was generally carefully polished with a spatula on the outside.

Although hidden designs were widespread from the seventh to the beginning of the eighth century, they gradually fell out of use. Still common in the late 740s, they had become quite rare by the late 760s and disappeared soon after that. The trend towards functionalism and resulting simplification in pottery was accelerating. This trend could be seen in terms of the manufacturing process as well, judging by the results of a careful reconstruction of the stages of the process. For example, a theory has been put forward suggesting that the making of one *tsuki* (up to the point just prior to firing) required five techniques and eleven steps in the early eighth century, three techniques and four steps during the later eighth century, two techniques and three steps at the beginning of the ninth century, and soon thereafter another step was eliminated. Procedures were simplified, designs eliminated. The potter's purpose became nothing more than to produce a utilitarian piece of tableware.

As we shall see in the next chapter, the population of Nara Capital must have been around 100,000. The birth of this ancient city also meant the creation of a huge concentration of consumers—a development with far-reaching effects on both agricultural and crafts production. There are written documents confirming that *haji* and *sue* ware were on sale in the markets of the capital. The change towards large-scale production for impersonal masses of urban consumers is reflected in the products themselves. Would all the pottery on sale to these urban consumers have been manufactured in a single location?

The techniques of *haji* manufacture described above have tended to vary greatly over time, but it seems that variation of a lesser degree may have existed even among the techniques of a single period. These variations, as well as the visible differences in the quality and composition of the clay, make it possible to divide the early eighth-century *haji* ware excavated in Nara Capital into two groups. Let us call them Groups 1 and 2. Nabunken's Sawada Masaaki has conducted compositional analyses of several samples from each of the two groups, using fluorescent X-ray analysis. In this method, each sample is first irradiated with X-rays. This stimulates the various elements in the sample to give off their own secondary X-rays—the fluorescent X-rays—of characteristic wave lengths. From the types and relative strengths of the secondary waves, it is possible to determine the identity and proportion of each element in the sample. One advantage of this method is that it does not damage the object being analysed. For this reason, it is the most widely used technique of compositional analysis where cultural properties are involved.

Using this method, the amount of strontium (Sr), rubidium (Rb), and zirconium

**50**
'Hidden design' on *haji* ware. Among the few decorated *haji* vessels of the Nara period, this 'hidden design' was particularly common.

(Zr) in each sample was measured. When the measurements were compared, there was a clear difference between samples belonging to each of the two groups of *haji* ware. These particular elements occur in the earth's crust only in traces, of the order of a hundredth of a per cent, and could not have been added to the soil by human agency. The conclusion is that the differences are due to the clay's having come from two different sources, and that the two groups of pottery were therefore possibly manufactured in different places. *Haji* ware sharing the features of Group 1 turns up frequently in excavations throughout Nara Prefecture. Pottery resembling Group 2, on the other hand, is uncommon in Nara Prefecture outside of Nara Capital itself, but occurs often in sites from Shiga and southern Kyoto Prefectures to the north of the capital. Apparently Nara Capital was supplied with ceramics from both north and south. Research of this kind is still in its infancy within the Nara Capital area, but it promises to be very fruitful.

The Engi Shiki procedures, describing the situation at the start of the tenth century, mentions several groups which supplied *haji* ware to Heian Capital as tax payments in kind. From Yamato Province there were the Nie-no-haji, the Tamate-no-haji, and an unnamed group who contributed ceramic cooking kettles. From Kawachi Province (the central region of modern Osaka Prefecture) there were the Tsukitsukuri-no-haji and a second Nie-no-haji group. Although scientific tests have not yet been conducted, observation with the naked eye suggests that some of the ceramics excavated in the capital may have come from Kawachi. It appears that the increasing specialization among potters had led to the emergence of clearly identified groups of artisans concentrated in a single location. Can this tenth-century situation be projected back into the eighth century? Judging from the ceramics themselves, it seems quite likely.

### Ceramic research: *Sue* ware and glazed wares

The identification of the probable site of the Jewelled Hall of the East Precinct was based partly on ceramic evidence. The *Shoku Nihongi* chronicle describes that hall as having had lapis-lazuli roof tiles, and a number of green and three-colour glazed tiles were indeed recovered from a likely area in the eastern palace grounds (see pl. 9). We also mentioned above that Pit SK820, which was filled in during the late 740s, contained not only large quantities of *sue* and *haji* ware but also a single small three-colour jar lid (pl. 10). Since the primary component of the glazes is lead, these glazed items are called lead-glazed ceramics. To refer more specifically to colour, we can speak of three-colour (glazed in yellow, green, and white) or two-colour ceramics, both of which are also called polychrome ceramics (pl. 11).

Lead-glazed ceramics were first produced in China and came into full flower with the Tang three-colour tradition. The technology of polychrome glazing spread northeast to the ancient realms of Bohai (in modern northeast China) and Silla (on the Korean Peninsula). The art was apparently brought to Japan by potters who were among the members of missions sent to Tang China, perhaps in 702 or at the latest as part of the 717 delegation. At any rate, it was around this time that state-controlled production of glazed ceramics must have begun in Japan. The technology may have been transmitted to Japan, but there remained great differences in quality between the Chinese and Japanese wares. In terms of colour, for example, Japanese polychrome pottery used only yellow, green, and white, whereas the Chinese had, in addition, a striking deep blue glaze. Presumably the Japanese did not have access to cobalt, the colouring agent in the blue glaze. Even the three colours which the Japanese did use could not match the transparent beauty of the Tang three-colour wares: in Japan they became dull and cloudy. This is most glaringly obvious with the white glaze, which contains no copper or iron. In Tang wares this is a colourless, exquisitely transparent glaze which allows the white of the potter's clay itself to show through; for Nara three-colour and other Japanese polychrome wares, we should perhaps rename this the 'muddy white glaze'. Decorations as well are much more elaborate on the Chinese examples. Sometimes a pattern would be stamped repeatedly over the surface of an object; or an appliqué of moulded clay would create a design in relief; or an entire vessel might be made in a mould, allowing for extremely delicate ornamental effects. Rich in variation, these Tang ceramics far surpassed the Nara three-colour wares and their simple shapes. The gorgeous, sumptuous Tang three-colour wares demonstrate the insatiable pursuit of the perfectly transparent 'white' glaze. The vastly simpler Nara three-colour wares, by contrast, were dressed mainly in green, with yellow and white as auxiliary hues. Although technical reasons may be the proximate cause of this difference in quality, we can perhaps also discern here the influence of differences in taste between Japan and China.

Tang three-colour wares were mostly intended as grave-goods, that is, they belonged to the land of the dead. Japanese polychrome ceramics, on the other hand, belonged to the living. They have most frequently been recovered from palaces, temples, and government offices, although some jars for holding cremated remains have also been found. Of course, being specially designed products, these polychrome wares generally occur only in small quantities. Moreover, although they have been found from northeastern Japan all the way down to Kyūshū, they are concentrated in the Nara and Osaka regions—the ancient centres of power and commerce—and most particularly in Nara Capital and Nara Palace. Most of these wares must have had one of two social functions: either to decorate Buddhist temples and Shintō shrines or to be used in the rituals conducted there, or to add colour to the daily lives of the aristocracy. It is thought that the only individuals who had access to polychrome pottery were aristocrats of the Fifth Rank and above (i.e., the upper fourteen steps on the thirty-step hierarchy). There were 125 such persons at the start of the eighth century, and a later expansion of the system did not increase the number to much above 200. Nara three-colour wares were indeed luxury goods. Ancient urbanization thus not only gave rise to the large-scale production of ceramics for a mass consumer market, it also led to a small-scale, specialized ceramic industry utilizing imported technology to satisfy the demands of a tiny elite.

During the eighth century, only lead-glazed ceramics were available, but a new ash-glazed pottery spread widely during the ninth century. Wood ash would be mixed with a quantity of potter's clay to form a glaze of a muddy consistency. Fired at something over 1240°C, the result was a hard, light green ware. Ash-glazed pottery was first produced near Mt. Sanage, located east of present-day Nagoya in

Aichi Prefecture. This region yielded a potter's clay, kaolin, of excellent quality which fired to a delicate white state. The availability of this clay later had an important influence on the emergence of medieval ceramic traditions such as Seto and Tokoname wares. Kaolin can withstand high firing temperatures, while lesser clays may warp. Production of a high-fired, hard ash-glazed ware began at the Sanage kilns.

These ash-glazed Sanage wares dominated the ceramic scene from the ninth to eleventh centuries, but some examples have been excavated at Nara Capital as well. In 1959, during the first full-scale excavations conducted by Nabunken at the Nara Palace site, digging was conducted at what was later identified as the probable site of the Great Catering Office. One pit at the site contained a sizeable concentration of discarded pottery from the early ninth century. This was the result of a short-lived attempt to revive the abandoned Nara Capital during the ninth century (see pp. 132–33). The pit was filled mostly with several thousand pieces of *haji* tableware. Since the pit was shallow and lay near the surface, these pieces changed to a reddish-grey colour and largely crumbled to bits. Among these *haji* sherds were the partial fragments of a 'flat jug', coated thickly on the exterior with a light green ash glaze. A flat jug is a type of very shallow container with a large flared spout rising from one side of its top surface. From the eighth century on, a handle was also attached on top, as in the one shown in plate 15. These flat, spouted jugs seem to have been intended to hold *sake*. The present specimen is of great interest, because other sherds from this same jug were found in a ditch some 60 metres away.

Several years prior to 1959, excavations had already been underway at the Sanage kiln site, the source of the original ash-glazed ceramics. Investigations at the site, at the southwest foot of Mt. Sanage, were led by Narasaki Shōichi of Nagoya University. The results of this work had gradually become known throughout the academic community; and it was surprising to learn that even during the Heian period, heretofore considered a relative vacuum in terms of ceramic history, such excellent pottery was being produced. Some of us working at Nara Palace had visited Nagoya to absorb the research results more thoroughly, and Narasaki had visited Nara Palace. It was during this time that the spouted jug was discovered. It was immediately recognized as a Sanage ash-glazed type. It would therefore appear that pottery from Owari (the province approximately coextensive with modern Aichi Prefecture) travelled as far as Yamato.

During these excavations in 1959, an assemblage of *sue* pottery was discovered in the 'extraction hole' of an embedded pillar. An extraction hole is a hole dug diagonally towards the base of an embedded pillar, to aid in its removal when a building is being dismantled (see fig. 9 *bottom left*). Once the pillar had been removed, pottery and wood scraps would frequently be tossed into the hole. Most of the *sue* items were the typical blue-grey jars and pots, presumably produced near the palace or else in the Kawachi region of modern Osaka Prefecture. There were also, however, two hard, grey-white long-necked jars. Judging from the material and technique, one of these was definitely from the Sanage kilns (fig. 51 *far left*). On the 'shoulder' of this otherwise quite smooth long-necked Sanage jar was a large, rough area. One view is that an ash glaze had originally been applied to that area but had fallen off during firing. More likely, though, this is an example of a *sue* vessel from a transitional stage before the ash-glaze technique had been completely adopted. The other long-necked jar (fig. 51 *second from right*) was judged to have come from the Sabu-kaze kilns in modern Okayama Prefecture. Sabukaze is the term used for a group of *sue* kiln remains which date from the Tumulus (300–710) up to the Nara period. The kilns lie near the large production region for Bizen ware, one of the major ceramic traditions of the early modern period. Nevertheless, the clay used in this Sabukaze jar has all the characteristics of the clay used at the distant Sanage kilns. These two long-necked *sue* jars are dated to the late eighth century, on the assumption that the building in question was torn down at that time.

Pottery excavated at the Nara Palace site includes not only the precursors of the early modern Seto and Bizen traditions. There are also pieces which may be considered to be the predecessors of Mino ware, another major early modern tradition. These are *sue* vessels with the place-name Mino stamped into them (fig. 52). Since 1966, two such vessels have been found within the palace grounds and two more elsewhere in the capital. The remains of the kilns that produced such stamped vessels have already been located, on a bluff overlooking the Nagara River, northeast of modern Gifu City (Gifu Prefecture). In all, more than 140 kilns have been discovered in the immediate area. *Sue* ware was produced here, in ancient Mino Province, from the fifth to the twelfth century. The kiln group has been given the name Mino-Sue. A few of these kilns were producing the Mino-stamped wares. These Mino-Sue wares, unlike the Sanage and Sabukaze products, had no particular distinguishing characteristics, whether in materials, technique, or shape. Without the stamp, it would be difficult to identify their place of origin.

It is of interest to note that the Seto, Bizen, and Mino areas, which were later to gain fame for their distinctive ceramic traditions, were already sending their wares to the capital in the eighth century in response to mass consumer demand. The

**51** *Sue* ware transported to Nara Palace. The vessels (from *left* to *right*) were manufactured respectively in: Sanage, 110 km northeast of Nara Capital; the vicinity of Nara Capital; Sabukaze, 150 km west of the capital; and 200 km east of the capital.

**52**
*Sue* ware bearing the stamp 'Mino'. Mino is a region 130 km northeast of Nara Capital. Goods were requisitioned from every region for Nara Palace, which had become a centre of massive consumption.

Sanage kilns are located 110 kilometres northeast of Nara, the Sabukaze kilns are 150 kilometres to the west, and the Mino-Sue kilns are about 40 kilometres northwest of Sanage.

The *haji*, *sue*, and polychrome wares discussed in this chapter constitute merely a tiny fraction of all the artifacts recovered from Nara Palace and Nara Capital. Nevertheless, the study of these few artifacts provides an indication of the overwhelming influence exerted by Nara Capital—ancient Japan's first major consumption centre—on the organization of craft production. The significance of the rise of ancient cities in Japan has already been discussed and debated from many angles. So far, though, insufficient consideration has been given to the impact of ancient urbanization on society as a whole. The abundant artifacts recovered from Nara hold the key to determining the nature of ancient cities and their many influences.

# Chapter 4

# Ancient Cities, Their Residents, and Urban Life

### The residences of the capital

In January 1979 a farmer in the village of Tawara was tilling his field, when he discovered a cremation grave accompanied by a bronze memorial plaque (fig. 53). The village, near the southeastern corner of modern Nara City and just beyond the mountains that form the eastern edge of the Nara Basin, lies 10 kilometres east-southeast of Nara Palace, not far from the ancient Nara Capital. According to the epitaph on the plaque, the remains were those of Ō-no-Yasumaro,* Lower Junior Fourth Rank, Fifth Order, formerly residing in 4th Jō, 4th Bō, Left Capital, deceased on the sixth day of the seventh month of the seventh year of Yōrō (723). Ō-no-Yasumaro was the compiler of the *Kojiki* (*Record of Ancient Matters*), which shares with the *Nihonshoki* (*Chronicle of Japan*) the distinction of being the oldest extant histories compiled in Japan. The discovery of the grave of the compiler of the *Kojiki* not only sent shock waves through the scholarly world, it also made the front-page headlines of newspapers throughout the country.

The location of 4th Jō, 4th Bō, Yasumaro's address according to the epitaph, can be pin-pointed on the reconstructed plan of Nara Capital, as we know it, through topographical evidence and archaeology (fig. 54). It lies just west of the central district of modern Nara, adjacent to the western edge of Japan Railway Nara Station. According to documentary sources, Nara-no-osa Musamaro (Upper Junior Eighth Rank) was registered in this same block in 745, as was Tamba-no-fuhito Azumando at about the same time. It is also recorded that Hozumi-no-ason Kako, who was promoted to Lower Junior Fifth Rank in 783, was from this block. However, although all four may have been registered in 4th Jō, 4th Bō, we have no proof that they actually lived there.** Since the block is some 510 metres square, it would in any case be impossible to locate their individual residences.

---

*In early Japan it was common to link the family and personal names with the genitive particle *no*. This practice is followed in modern Japan when referring to ancient personages.

**It was only few decades earlier that, with the emergence of the ancient urban capitals, a significant number of people had begun to reside elsewhere than in the community of their birth, and at first the registration system was unable to reflect this fact clearly. It cannot therefore be assumed that the place of registration and the place of residence are the same.

Nara Capital, as noted in Chapter 1, is cut into a pattern resembling a chessboard by a series of major roads (ōji; lit. 'large road') running east-west and north-south (see fig. 2). Each 'square' on the board has a two-element address. Numbering from north to south, the squares are called 1st Jō, 2nd Jō . . . on up to 9th Jō. Looking at a map, it may be seen that all the squares in a single east-west, 'horizontal' row have the same Jō address; we will therefore translate Jō as 'Row'. East-west orientation is measured from Scarlet Phoenix Avenue, the capital's main street which runs north-south through its centre. Moving away from Scarlet Phoenix Avenue both to the east (Left Capital) and to the west (Right Capital), the columns of blocks are numbered 1st Bō, 2nd Bō, and so forth. We can translate Bō as 'Column'. The overall address, then, must specify the district plus the row and column number, as in Left Capital, 4th Row, 4th Column. The directions 'left' and 'right' in this case are from the viewpoint of the emperor, looking south from his palace at the capital's northern edge.

Each of these large blocks is usually crossed in both horizontal and vertical directions by three smaller roads (kōji; lit. 'small road'). We shall refer to the larger roads (ōji) as Avenues and the smaller ones (kōji) as Streets, capitalizing them to avoid confusion. The Avenues derive their names from the adjacent Rows or Columns. The east-west Avenues are named after the Row immediately to the north: 3rd Row Avenue lies immediately south of 3rd Row. (The exceptions are the Avenues adjacent to 1st Row; the one above 1st Row, at the northern edge of the capital, is called 1st Row North Avenue, while the one below this Row is 1st Row South Avenue.) The north-south Avenues are named after the adjacent Column closest to Scarlet Phoenix Avenue, with a prefix to specify the side of Scarlet Phoenix Avenue on which they lie. Thus the Avenue to the west of *Right* Capital, 3rd Column is named West 3rd Column Avenue, but the one to the west of *Left* Capital, 3rd Column is named East 2nd Column Avenue.

The criss-crossing of the three Streets in each direction divides each large block into sixteen sub-blocks. These are assigned numbers from 1 to 16 (see fig. 54). In each half of the capital, the northernmost sub-block nearest to Scarlet Phoenix Avenue is called Sub-block 1. Numbering proceeds south until Sub-block 4, then north in the adjacent column of sub-blocks, then south in the next, and so forth; thus Sub-block 16 is in the northeast corner of each block in the eastern half of the capital but in the northwest corner in the western half. Each sub-block has an area of 1 *chō*, but how large is a *chō?*

The distance between the centres of two adjacent Avenues was a uniform 1,800 *shaku* (or 1,500 large *shaku;* 530.5 metres). The distance between the centre lines of a Street and either of its adjacent roads (whether an Avenue or another Street) was a consistent 450 *shaku*. However, since the Avenues were considerably wider than the Streets, a sub-block facing an Avenue had in effect to sacrifice more of its area to the road surface and was consequently much smaller than other sub-blocks. The Streets were from 6 to 7 metres wide, while the Avenues ranged from a width of 16 metres to 75 in the case of Scarlet Phoenix Avenue. Thus, although all sub-blocks were defined as being 1 *chō* in area, the actual area ranged from less than a hectare to around 1.5 hectares. In most cases, these sub-blocks were divided further into lots suitable for a single residence.

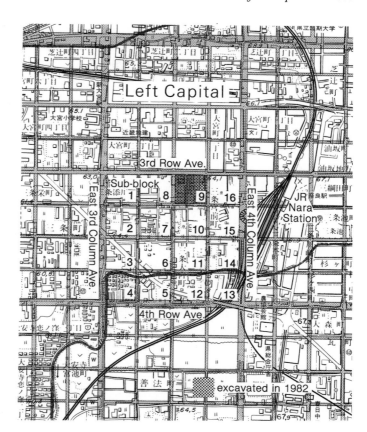

**53** *(left)* The memorial plaque of Ō-no-Yasumaro. Ō-no-Yasumaro was the compiler of the eighth-century *Kojiki* chronicle. The grave containing his cremated remains was discovered in 1979, and this plaque, 65 cm in length, accompanied it.

**54** *(right)* The present appearance around Left Capital, 4th Row, 4th Column. The address inscribed on Ō-no-Yasumaro's memorial plaque is now situated west of the Japan Railway Nara Station.

Excavation has shown that Scarlet Phoenix Avenue is oriented barely a quarter of a degree (15′41″) west of its intended direction of true north. The directional deviation over a distance of 1 kilometre would have been a mere 4.5 metres. True north was presumably calculated by measuring the sun's path. From what we have reconstructed of ancient Japanese measuring technology, this represents an astonishing degree of accuracy. Methods for determining direction via astronomical measurement, for the purpose of orienting buildings, were imported from the continent towards the end of the sixth century and spread in connection with the erection of the first Buddhist temples. Oddly, despite the precision in measuring the north-south axis, right angles were usually inaccurate by a margin ranging from 4 to 11 degrees. Techniques for drawing a perpendicular line were not well understood.

In the days of Fujiwara Capital, Nara's predecessor, an imperial edict of 691 specified the size of house lots to be granted to nobles of various ranks (many, though not all, of whom were government officials). The Minister of the Right was to receive 4 *chō;* holders of the Fourth Rank and above, 2 *chō;* members of the Fifth Rank, 1 *chō*. (The Nara period terminology for ranks is employed here for convenience; Fujiwara terminology was somewhat different.) Nobility of the Sixth Rank and lower, as well as people of no rank, received land according to household size: 1 *chō* for large families, 1/2 *chō* for medium-size families, and 1/4 *chō* for small families. Another document specified the criteria for determining household size: a large family was one with eight or more adolescent or adult males, a medium family had four to seven, and a small family had two or three. (The situation for households with only one adult male is unclear, but there appear to have been few such cases.) Another document concerning house lot allotments survives from Naniwa Capital and is dated 734. It states that Second Rank officials and higher received at least 1 *chō*, Third to Fifth Ranks received a maximum of 1/2 *chō*, and Sixth Rank and below were to get no more than 1/4 *chō*. These amounts were less than half of those in effect at Fujiwara. Today there are several opinions as to the layout of Naniwa Capital, but the majority view is that it was approximately the same size as Fujiwara Capital or perhaps even half as large again. Apparently, then, the shrinkage in allotment standards was not due to a loss of land. It has been suggested that the population may have increased significantly during those forty-three years and that the size of allotments had to be reduced accordingly. It may be fruitless to pursue the matter on the basis of such evidence. For one thing, a provisional calculation of the number of rank-holders at Fujiwara Capital reveals that there was not enough land within the capital to adhere to the allotment terms in any case. Thus the allotment edicts may have been no more than proposals which were never carried out.

No such edicts survive for Nara Capital. Moreover, there are only a very few actual cases in which we know how much land a certain person had. Among these are the mansions of Fujiwara Fuhito and Prince Niitabe. When the capital moved to Nara, Fujiwara Fuhito (659–720) was Minister of the Right with the Senior Second Rank. His daughter Miyako had married Emperor Monmu, and another daughter Kōmyō was to become the consort of Emperor Shōmu. It was Fuhito who established the Fujiwara family at the head of the nobility of ancient Japan. Prince Niitabe was the seventh son of Emperor Tenmu. Imperial princes were ranked according to four orders, First Order being the highest. Niitabe was a Third Order prince when the capital moved to Nara, but he had ascended to the top order by 724. After Fuhito's death, Niitabe took power over the military and was at the centre of the political arena as well. He died in 735. Both of these men, then, would surely have been at the highest point on any scale of house lot allotments.

According to historical sources, Fuhito's mansion later became Hokkeji temple (mentioned frequently in previous chapters), while Prince Niitabe's mansion was donated to Tōshōdaiji temple in the west central part of the capital. Excavations at each of these temples has revealed a sizeable complex of embedded-pillar buildings, which lends support to the documentary evidence. Hokkeji is posited to have once occupied more than 4 *chō* of land; and so if Fuhito's mansion was converted directly into a temple with little alteration, then presumably it also covered more than 4 *chō*. Tōshōdaiji also covers some 4 *chō* of land, and excavations suggest that the main portion of the prince's mansion covered at least the northern 2 *chō* of the temple grounds.

There is evidence of at least one noble who had considerably larger grounds than these. This is Fujiwara Nakamaro (706–64), Fuhito's grandson. Enjoying the confidence of his aunt, the imperial consort Kōmyō, he achieved great political power, was appointed Prime Minister and rose to the Senior First Rank. Later, he led an unsuccessful rebellion in an attempt to oust the powerful Buddhist priest Dōkyō, favourite of the retired Empress Kōken, and for his treasonous acts was captured and beheaded. The current dominant opinion is that Nakamaro's mansion occupied the 8 *chō* in the eastern half of Left Capital, 4th Row, 2nd Column. Archaeological evidence supports this view.

Considering the above three cases together, we can conclude that if there was a house lot allotment scheme in effect at Nara Capital, then its provisions must have been similar to those recorded in the Fujiwara Capital document, at least for high-ranking aristocratic officials. The total land area available for housing at Nara was more than three times as much as that at Fujiwara, so even if there had been a slight increase in the urban population, it should have been possible to adhere to standards close to those promulgated at Fujiwara.

Let us return to Ō-no-Yasumaro. When the capital moved to Nara, he had already achieved the Fifth Rank; at his death in 723, he was head of the Ministry of Civil Affairs and held the Lower Junior Fourth Rank. The Ministry of Civil Affairs was in charge of the census and taxes. Since there were only eight ministries, their heads were very powerful. According to the standards of the Fujiwara edict, Yasumaro's private mansion would have occupied more than 1 *chō*. As mentioned above, the size of a *chō* varied somewhat within the capital, but in Yasumaro's neighbourhood it would have been approximately 120 metres square.

In 1982, excavations were carried out in one of the sub-blocks of Left Capital, 4th Row, 4th Column—the address recorded on Yasumaro's memorial plaque. According to the system of numbering the sixteen sub-blocks, this area in the north-centre of the block was Sub-block 9 (see fig. 54). Unlike the excavations within the palace grounds proper, almost all investigations elsewhere in the capital are so-called 'rescue excavations'. These are excavations carried out in the face of rapidly encroaching development, for the purpose of at least documenting the sub-surface situation prior to its total destruction through construction activities. The 'opposite' of a rescue excavation is an academic excavation. The latter is carefully planned to provide evidence concerning a specific hypothesis by digging in an area chosen in relation to the problem.

At present, over 95 per cent of all excavations in Japan are of the rescue type— some 10,000 annually, and increasing year by year. In contrast, the annual number of academic excavations is about 350. Sadly, even within Nara Capital (as opposed to Nara Palace) there are virtually no academic excavations going on at present. The number of rescue excavations has increased since the late 1960s, but they depend of course on the vagaries of development. Thus, although some 1,000 excavations have been conducted to date, not a single sub-block has yet been completely excavated. The scope of investigation is usually confined to the area to be occupied by the new structure.

The excavation in Yasumaro's block was limited to 620 square metres—the planned size of a new private school building. This area in the northwestern part of Sub-block 9 constituted less than 4 per cent of the whole sub-block. Nevertheless, the investigation revealed several important clues for reconstructing the Nara period land allotment scheme: traces of pillared buildings, board fences, ditches, and roads. For example, a ditch dated to the early eighth century ran east-west across the sub-block, one-fourth of the distance from its northern edge towards its southern edge. It appears to be the moat of a residence. If we assume that the entire area to the north of the moat belonged to a single mansion, then its area would have been 1/4 *chō* and its dimensions 30 metres north-south and 125 metres east-west. It seems strange, though, to choose to divide a sub-block into four narrow strips rather than into four square plots for housing. Thus it is likely that this northern strip is further divided in two by a north-south boundary somewhat to the east of the excavated region; in other words, the house lot in question is actually the upper half of the northwest quadrant of the sub-block. In that case, this residence would have occupied only 1/8 *chō*.

Towards the middle of the century, however, the boundary moat mentioned above disappeared amid a major reorganization of the divisions in Sub-block 9. Although the overall pattern is unknown, it appears that this area was now incorporated into a plot of either a half or a whole *chō*. Its buildings were systematically laid out, and board fences separated different sections of the grounds. At the end of the Nara period, though, the grounds apparently shrank back to the earlier boundaries, as indicated by a board fence running along the line where the original southern boundary moat had lain.

Accepting that Ō-no-Yasumaro lived somewhere in this block, we still have absolutely no idea in which of the sixteen sub-blocks his residence stood. Even the identity of the occupants of Sub-block 9 remains a total mystery. All we know is that there is a good possibility that a high-ranking official lived here during the middle years of the century, when the lot probably had an area of a half to a whole *chō*.

Of all the excavations in Nara Capital so far, a scant thirty have yielded clues to the system of apportioning land for houses. One reason, as mentioned above, is that virtually all excavations outside of the palace have been rescue jobs, meaning that the site cannot be freely selected by the archaeologists, and the scale is almost sure to be small. Limited resources have made it necessary in any case to select only a limited number of construction sites for excavation, and until very recently the tendency has been to choose those sites likely to contribute to our understanding of the layout of the streets, in order to clarify the overall city plan. Thus, rather than the centre of the sub-blocks, it has generally been only their edges—where they border on roads—that have received attention from researchers. Moreover, the thirty excavations which have cast light on housing land apportionment have been predominantly in the north of the capital, near the palace. Only a few such excavations have been conducted in the central and southern districts; 6th and 7th Rows in particular have remained untouched. At present, we have no choice but to base our hypotheses about such land allotment on these thirty potentially unrepresentative cases.

The smallest lot size mentioned in the Fujiwara Capital housing land allotment edict was 1/4 *chō*. House lots smaller than this have been discovered at Nara Capital, but to date none have been found further north than 4th Row, where Ō-no-Yasumaro was registered. Lots smaller than 1/8 *chō* have been found only in Yasumaro's block (4th Row, 4th Column) and in 8th Row—again, only in the capital's southern region. Conversely, all cases in which a lot of 1 *chō* or more survived undissected throughout the Nara period are in 3rd Row and above. As for lots of 1 *chō* or larger which at some time were subdivided, these are all in the 5th Row or further north (fig. 55 *top*). A pattern seems to be emerging. The northern part of the capital, near the palace, was occupied by mansions whose grounds covered 1 *chō* or more. Moving further to the south, away from the palace, smaller allotments begin to appear: from about 5th Row, some lots of 1/4 *chō*; in the southernmost third of the capital, lots of 1/8 *chō* or even smaller. (5th Row, incidentally, lay exactly halfway between the capital's northern and southern borders.) Unfortunately, there are as yet no data from 6th, 7th, and 9th Rows.

If we provisionally apply the Fujiwara Capital housing land allotment edict to Nara, we may suggest that nobles of the Fifth Rank and above—those receiving 1 *chō* or more—resided in the 5th Row or further north. This hypothesis is on the whole supported by the documentary evidence.

Of people known to have resided (or at least been registered) in Nara Capital, there are only 110 of whom we know both the names and addresses. Of these, 51 were persons of rank. Persons of the Fifth Rank or higher all lived in 5th Row or above (fig. 55 *bottom*). For those of lower rank, the situation was less clear-cut: some people of the Sixth Rank or lower also resided in 5th Row or above. There is a record, for example, of the buying and selling of slaves* in 748 by a certain Ōhara-no-mahito Imaki, a member of the Lower Senior Seventh Rank who was registered in Left Capital, 1st Row, 3rd Column. This block lay very close to the palace's north-eastern edge. It is difficult to believe that a person of the Seventh Rank could live so close to the palace. Indeed, this was no ordinary lower-ranking functionary but a member of the royal family: Emperor Tenmu's grandson, Prince Imaki, who eventually ascended to the Upper Junior Fifth Rank. The location of his residence was appropriate to his status. But there were also some apparent commoners of no rank living north of 5th Row. No doubt most of these were the retainers or servants of nobles and higher-ranking officials living in the area. Thus there was apparently no particular stricture against people of the Sixth Rank or lower, or even against people of no rank living north of 5th Row. It is therefore more relevant to focus on the absence of people of the higher ranks in the southern part of the capital.

Despite the paucity of both archaeological and documentary data, the fact that these two types of data agree so well encourages us to accept two inferences: that we are safe in drawing on the Fujiwara Capital housing land allotment edict as evidence for the situation at Nara Capital; and that it is highly probable, despite some exceptions, that people registered in a given block of the capital actually resided in that location.

---

*Slaves could be bought and sold and were not allowed to choose their own dwellings. Marriage, however, seems to have been free; if the mother was a slave, the child would also become one. The owner did not have the right to kill a slave. Only the emperor could grant freedom. An estimated 5 to 10 per cent of the populace fell into this category.

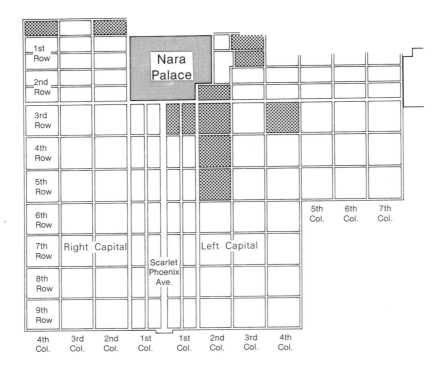

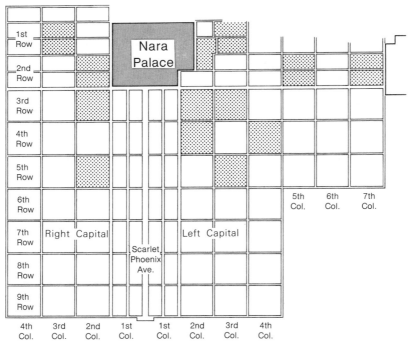

**55** Excavation locations of mansions more than 1 *chō* in area (*top*), and residential locations revealed in documentary sources for aristocrats above the Fifth Rank (*bottom*).

## Great mansions and smaller dwellings

In Chapter 1 we described how excavations in the palace's eastern projection revealed traces of a large garden with a pond, artificial streams, and even a pillared
building beside the pond (see pp. 28–29). In 1975 the remains of a similarly impressive garden was discovered not far from the palace. The location was about
1 kilometre east-southeast of the palace's Chiisako Gate, in the centre of Sub-block 6
of Left Capital, 3rd Row, 2nd Column. Excavation of more than 35 per cent of the
sub-block has revealed that, throughout the Nara period, Sub-block 6 formed part
of a large estate of 1 *chō* or perhaps even of several *chō*. Directly in the middle of this
sub-block was a garden with an approximately S-shaped pond (figs. 56, 58, pl. 4).

Since investigations had to be confined to the pond and its immediate surroundings, much is still unknown about the overall layout of Sub-block 6 and the estate
of which it was a part. According to our best surmise at present, a board fence
separated the pond area from the northern and eastern thirds of the sub-block; and
to the north of the fence were various sheds and a well, while the area to the east
seems to have been largely an open space devoid of buildings. The important part
of the compound was the area to the southwest of the fence, with the S-shaped
pond occupying its northeast quadrant. To the west of the pond were the principal
buildings; the situation to the south is unknown.

Prior to the construction of Nara Capital, the area of this sub-block was cut by a
river flowing south from its northeast corner. When the capital was built, the river
was re-routed into a canal which formed the eastern border of Sub-block 6, in accord-
ance with the Row-Column system. To draw water from this river into the pond,
a watercourse some 4 to 6 metres wide was constructed along the former riverbed,
ending near the pond's northern edge. The pond and watercourse were connected
by a wooden conduit (fig. 56, views A, B). The conduit was a square timber 5
metres long with a channel dug out of its upper side. The channel was 12 centimetres wide and 10 centimetres deep and was covered with a wooden lid. But this
conduit and the watercourse were not in fact directly linked. How, then, did the
water reach the pond? It appears that there was a 15-centimetre hole in the lid of
the conduit, towards the end nearest the watercourse. The water could have been
scooped manually into the conduit, but the hole was so small that most of the ladled
water would have spilled onto the ground. There must have been some device to increase the efficiency of the transfer. On the ground to each side of the conduit, near
where the hole in the lid would have been, traces of a post 15 centimetres square
(view B) were found. Perhaps a water trough was suspended between these two
posts in such a way that water ladled into it was funnelled directly through the hole
in the lid.

The southern end of the conduit led directly into the pond. The northern end of
the pond was separated from the rest by a barrier of good-sized rocks (view C). This
may have served as a sort of settling pool. Water from the conduit accumulated
here, the sediment settled on the bottom and only the purer water at the top eventually flowed into the main part of the pond. The conduit and most of the settling
pool actually lay to the north of the board fence which demarcated the
northern third of Sub-block 6. People seated or strolling along the edge of the

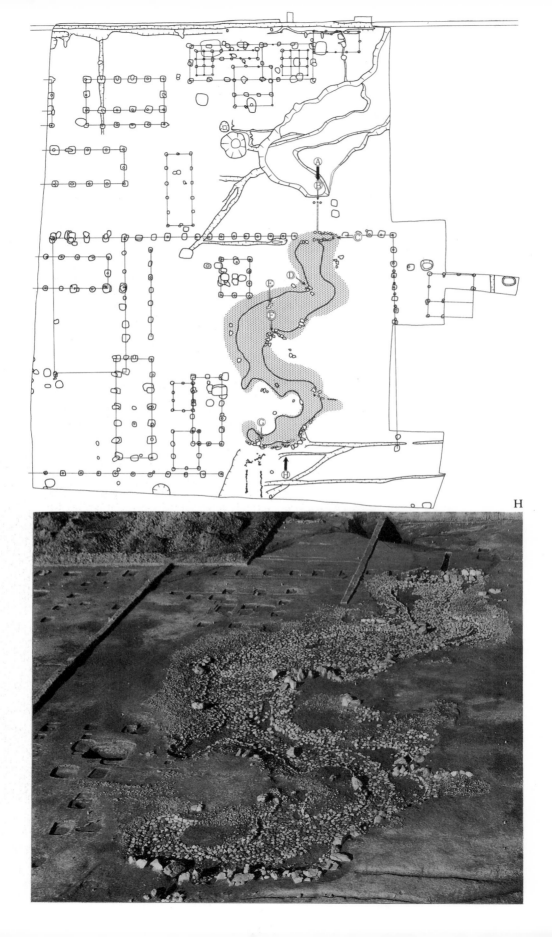

H

**56** Views of the garden at Sub-block 6 of Left Capital, 3rd Row, 2nd Column. A garden with a pond occupied the centre of North Palace Garden Mansion, which stood on a 1.5 ha lot. The pond has been reconstructed, thereby providing a unique opportunity to experience an eighth-century garden.

clear pond south of the fence would not have been able to see the workers ladling the water into the conduit.

The serpentine pond had an overall length of 55 metres. Its shoreline was quite varied in contour, so that the width ranged from 2 to 5 or 6 metres. The average depth was a shallow 20 centimetres, and even the deepest point was only 25 centimetres. The engineering of the pond was extremely elaborate. Both the shoreline and the bottom of the pond were lined with rounded stones (view D). Head- and fist-size stones supported the banks, while larger garden rocks of granite or andesite were distributed here and there around the shoreline (view F). There was a small sandy beach, and various large rocks stood in the water to represent islands (view D). At the pond's southern end was yet another wooden conduit—this time leading down from the bottom of the pond (view G). In the section of its lid which would have been visible below the water, there was a hole 12 centimetres in diameter. Removing a plug from this hole would allow the entire pond to be drained. In addition, there was an overflow trough leading to a separate rock-lined area. A line drawn to the mouth of this overflow trough from the spot where water flowed into the pond would have a downward gradient of about 1:300, that is, about 1 centimetre of vertical drop per 3 metres. Thus the pond would have had a gentle southward current.

At two places in the pond, angular wooden boxes lay submerged near the shore, embedded among the stones paving the pond bed (view E). Filled with dirt, these served as planters for aquatic plants. Cones of black pine and the seeds of plum, peach, and sandalwood have been found in the pond, as well as the leaves and branches of aquatic or waterside plants.

The cultivation of plants was obviously a central feature of a garden. Remains of plants—seeds, leaves, roots, etc.—have been recovered from various gardens in the palace and capital, and research is also being carried out on the many types of pollen found in the sediment on the bottom of ponds such as this one. These researches have been combined with botanical references in eighth-century poetic anthologies such as the *Man'yōshū* to yield a picture of the plant life of a Nara period garden. Most of these trees and flowers are still found in Japanese gardens today: pine, plum and peach trees, fringed pinks, orchids, plume grass, and so forth. Some, however, such as the mandarin orange and damson, have become much less common since then, while others such as the umbrella pine, wistaria, and five-needle pine which today seem indispensable were rare or absent. Nevertheless, it is interesting to find evidence in this early period of the Japanese love for plants, as well as of the tendency to create formal gardens of trees and flowers.

A slow current flowed through the shallow, narrow serpentine pond. Garden rocks lay here and there, garden trees dotted the shore, water plants adorned the pond's surface. To specialists in early Japanese literature, the setting may call to mind the Banquet of the Meandering Stream. This banquet finds its origins in the ancient Chinese custom of purifying oneself by a flowing stream on a ritually significant day in the third month (early April). By China's Six Dynasties period (the 3rd to 6th centuries), this had become formalized into a quasi-ritual social occasion held on the third day of the third month. People would gather to improvise poems and to float cups of wine on a stream. The *Shoku Nihongi* chronicle tells us that on the third day of the third month of the fifth year of Shinki (728) Emperor Shōmu held a Banquet of the Meandering Stream at a spot called Bird Pond Dyke. Several Chinese-style poems composed by participants on that occasion are recorded in the Japanese anthology *Kaifūsō*, compiled in 751.

The waterways, or raceways, for floating the *sake* cups during these banquets could have one of two profiles. In one type, the water flows from point A to point B, ending up some distance from its starting point. We may call this the *downstream* type. The other is the *circulating* type, which forms a continuous but meandering loop (fig. 57). Both types have been discovered in China. On the Korean Peninsula, a famous example has been found at the Abalone Rock Pavilion (Posŏk-chŏng) in Kyŏngju, for use by the kings of Silla. It is a classic example of the circulating type. By this typology, the pond-cum-raceway in Sub-block 6 of Left Capital, 3rd Row, 2nd Column is a downstream type. In fact, all Japanese examples, from raceways in gardens of the early modern period to those which serve today as tourist attractions, are of this type. Perhaps we have succeeded in tracing the Japanese tradition of downstream raceways all the way back to the eighth century.

The garden with this spectacular stone-lined pond at its heart was fenced off to the north and east and bordered by buildings to the west. Almost all of these buildings had their longer sides oriented north-south. By contrast, the less imposing buildings which lay to the north of the fence but south of the northernmost Street in Sub-block 6 were virtually all oriented east-west. In other residences excavated in the capital so far, the major buildings were overwhelmingly east-west in orientation. The exception in the present case is doubtless because the buildings

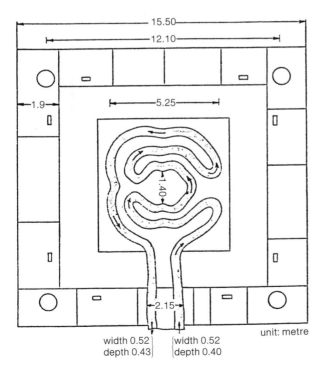

width 0.52
depth 0.43

width 0.52
depth 0.40

unit: metre

**57**
A 'meandering stream' waterway of the circulating type. Waterways used for the Banquet of the Meandering Stream could be either of the 'circulating' or, as in the North Palace Garden Mansion, of the 'downstream' type.

were laid out to face the garden to their east. If one stands among the traces of these buildings and looks towards the former garden, the mountains along the eastern edge of the Nara Basin loom impressively in the background (title page). It is almost as if the 'borrowed view' technique were already being practised in the eighth century. This is a technique familiar from Japanese gardens of the early modern period, whereby a garden is intended to be viewed as a part of the scenery in the background—hills, mountains, field—as if the garden and the distant objects were truly contiguous. It is highly probable that from these buildings one could indeed experience garden and mountains as a single landscape, despite the intervening board fence or tamped-earth wall. Of course, these mountains were surely visible from anywhere in the capital: the view was not unique to this particular garden. On the other hand, if the buildings had been situated directly to the north or south of the garden, the mountains would hardly have struck the eye at all. In this sense, we must credit the ancient landscape engineer with having taken the first step towards the later technique of the borrowed view, however undeveloped his art might otherwise be by comparison with his early modern period counterpart.

Many *mokkan* were recovered from the archaeological features of Sub-block 6, chiefly from the bed of the garden's northern waterway (the old rivercourse). Two of these bore the words 'North Palace'; and both appear to have been shipping tags for goods sent to that destination. According to documentary sources, a certain imperial princess named Kibi dwelt in a mansion called the North Palace. Another tablet seems to refer to the purchasing of food for the emperor. There is also a pot with the word 'chamberlain' inked on it. It is a chamberlain's duty to be in constant attendance on the emperor. This pot was presumably used by the chamberlain. All of these inscriptions point to a close connection between this garden and the emperor or someone very close to him. There are also the roof tiles. In general, the tiles unearthed in the capital bear different designs from those found within the palace grounds proper, but the tiles of the buildings in this garden are of the same type as the tiles at the palace; they were made at a government factory. Moreover, the Banquet of the Meandering Stream, which was probably held in this garden, was at this time still an important state ritual rather than mere entertainment. All in all, it is reasonable to suppose that this garden complex served as an outlying auxiliary palace to the main Nara Palace, or at least that it was the residence of an imperial prince or other top-ranking noble.

The excavation in Sub-block 6 of Left Capital, 3rd Row, 2nd Column was a rescue investigation prior to the erection of a new building for the Nara Central Post Office. With the discovery of such important archaeological features, however, the building plans were changed and the area was designated for preservation as a National Historic Site. A new municipal Historic Site Cultural Centre was built on its northern half, but the pond area and one of the western buildings have been reconstructed to form the only extant eighth-century garden (fig. 58, pl. 4 *bottom*).

Outside the palace, garden features have been discovered in only five locations in the capital. It may be significant that all of them are in the northern district, in 3rd Row or above. Once again we see a glimpse of apparent qualitative differences, reflecting status divisions, between the residences of the capital's southern sector and its northern part closer to the palace (fig. 59).

Let us refer to the complex of features in Sub-block 6, of which the garden is a major element, as the North Palace Garden Mansion site. Just north of this site— above the new Historic Site Cultural Centre—runs one of the principal east-west highways of Nara City, Ōmiya (lit. 'Great Palace') Road. In the days of Nara Capital, this was 3rd Row Middle Street, which lay halfway between 2nd Row and 3rd Row Avenues and split the blocks of 3rd Row into northern and southern halves. To the northeast of the Cultural Centre, north of Ōmiya Road, is Nara City Hall. It was built on land from the same block as the North Palace Garden Mansion, namely, Left Capital, 3rd Row, 2nd Column. The City Hall grounds en-compass all of the former Sub-blocks 15 and 16 as well as small parts of Sub-blocks 9 and 10. The previous City Hall had stood in the old city centre, but the need for additional floor space forced a move to the western, 'new district' of Nara where open land was available. In 1974, before building began, archaeological studies were made in Sub-blocks 15 and 10, for these were the locations where the present City Hall would stand. As it happened, attention was focused on Sub-block 15, and approximately 40 per cent of the entire sub-block was eventually excavated.

Throughout the Nara period, Sub-block 15 constituted a single, self-contained mansion and grounds (fig. 60). All the buildings were embedded-pillar structures oriented east-west. It is likely that the front entrance to the grounds was on the south side. The sub-block was split by a board fence into eastern and western halves, each of which had one particularly large building in its northern half. These were presumably the residences of the owner and his family. North of these two buildings, the dividing fence came to an end and a number of smaller structures were found. No doubt the remains of other small buildings lie undiscovered in the

**58** Reconstructed buildings of the North Palace Garden Mansion. One building and the garden at the North Palace have been reconstructed, the former at a cost of 118.5 million yen.

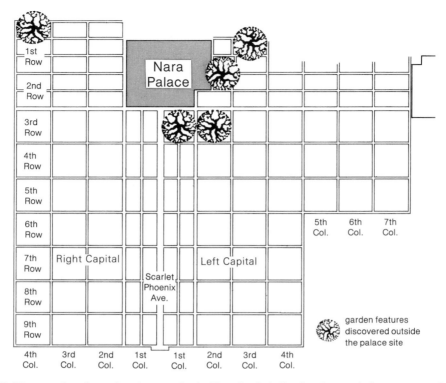

**59** Discovery locations of garden remains in Nara Capital. Gardens have only been excavated at locations in the northern third of Nara Capital. This is where the large mansions having such gardens were concentrated.

unexcavated areas. These smaller structures would have been kitchens and sheds, servants' quarters, and so forth. To the south of the large building in the western half was another board fence to provide privacy. Still other buildings lay to its south. Perhaps these were for receiving visitors who entered by the main south gate. Apart from the two largest buildings, almost all the other structures were a mere three posts wide and would have had simple gabled roofs. The basic core of each of the two large buildings was also a three-pillar gabled section, but each had been extended by additional sections. In one case, an additional row of pillars was added on either side, making a total width of five pillars. In the other, an additional row of pillars was added on all four sides, and the roof was either hip-gabled or hipped. Most of the structures at this site had been rebuilt one or more times, but in each case the basic plan remained almost the same.

The two main buildings had each been rebuilt twice. Their roofs of organic material were replaced with tiles during the latter half of the century. The other buildings apparently remained shingled with wood or bark, or possibly thatched, throughout the century. The roof tiles were of types which were either unknown or very rare at Nara Palace; in this, they differ from those at the North Palace Garden Mansion site. This suggests that the mansion at Sub-block 15, while it must have belonged to a very important and high-ranking official, was nevertheless a 'normal'

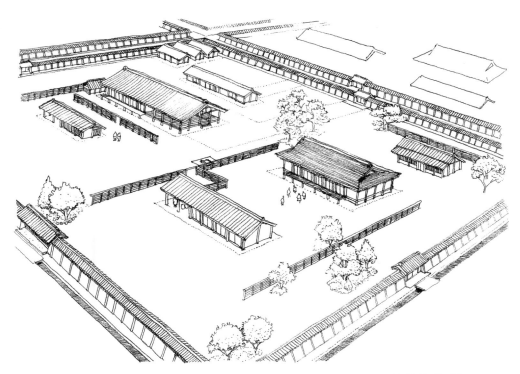

**60** Reconstruction of a mansion discovered in building the new Nara City Hall. Half a kilometre southeast of Nara Palace, this mansion excavated at Left Capital, 3rd Row, 2nd Column, Sub-block 15 is a typical example of a high-class residence of that era.

residence rather than some sort of auxiliary palace. Also, despite the fence which divides most of the sub-block into two halves, the fact that the fence disappears at both its northern and southern ends, together with the apparent existence of only a single well—an indispensable item for any residence—suggests that the entire sub-block did indeed constitute a single residential unit.

Mansions such as this, which occupied an entire sub-block, would have an area of 1 *chō*—about 14,000 square metres on average. Excavation in the capital has also revealed examples of residences at the bottom end of the size scale, built on lots of 1/8 or 1/16 *chō*.

Left Capital, 8th Row, 3rd Column is some 3 kilometres from Nara Palace; only 9th Row lies between it and the southern edge of the capital. This was the location of the public market known as the East Market. (A West Market stood in the same position in Right Capital.) The dominant theory is that the East Market occupied Sub-blocks 5, 6, 11, and 12 in the south-central part of the block. It had also been suggested that the East Horikawa River flowed through the market's eastern half, one-fourth of the way from its eastern edge, in other words, it split Sub-blocks 11 and 12 into eastern and western halves. In 1975, in advance of the construction of a large prefectural housing project, excavations were carried out in Sub-blocks 9, 10, 15, and 16, just to the northeast of the supposed market site. This was one of the few excavations in the southern half of the capital which yielded data relevant to residential patterns.

Let us summarize the results of this excavation, focusing on the situation in Sub-block 9 (see fig. 2). The East Horikawa River, 10 metres wide and 2 metres deep, cut Sub-block 9 into eastern and western halves. To the east of this sub-block was Sub-block 16, and to its south, immediately adjacent to the market, was Sub-block 10. Between Sub-block 9 and each of these sub-blocks was a Street some 6 metres wide. Between these two Streets and the river was the eastern half of Sub-block 9. The excavation dealt with the southernmost five-eighths of this eastern portion (fig. 61). Within this section, an interesting structural fact emerged. At various times during the course of the century, a series of east-west ditches separated the district into either fourths or eighths. If we assume that these ditches marked the northern and southern boundaries of house lots, and that their eastern and western boundaries were marked by the Street and the East Horikawa River respectively, then the lots would have had an area of 1/8 *chō* (when the ditches divided the north-south dimension into fourths) or 1/16 *chō* (when the division was into eighths). In each of these rectangular lots were a few buildings and a single well. Since the river lay to the west, the main entry into these lots must have been from the Street to the east. Each of the wells was in the eastern part of the lot, towards the main entrance. It is difficult to determine the number of buildings because of incomplete excavation, but on the lots of 1/8 *chō* there seem to have been five or six, and on the 1/16 *chō* lots a mere two or three. All were non-tiled, embedded-pillar structures. Let us refer to this area as the East Market Northeast Residential District site.

In the Fujiwara Capital housing land allotment edict, the smallest lot mentioned was 1/4 *chō*. At Naniwa the lower limit was smaller than that. We have just seen that at Nara some lots were as small as 1/16 *chō;* in fact, recent excavations have revealed lots of 1/32 *chō*, furnished with a well and a single building. On average, 1/32 *chō* is about 450 square metres. The existence of plots of this diminutive size had already been foreseen through a study of written sources. Among these sources was a document in connection with the borrowing of money from a bureau by a low-ranking official—one of several such documents to survive. In 773 this particular official borrowed 600 *mon*, offering as collateral his house lot of 1/32 *chō* with its two single-roofed buildings, located in Left Capital, 8th Row, 4th Column. Incidentally, the monthly interest on this loan was 15 per cent, or 90 *mon*. There is a notation on the document to the effect that the loan was repaid after three months in the amount of 870 *mon*.

It is clear that there were indeed house lots as small as 1/32 *chō*. A few doubts remain, however, as to whether such a lot could really have been intended to accommodate an entire family unit. Let us consider the case of the East Market Northeast Residential District. The suspected boundary markers between properties were the east-west ditches. These were extremely shallow and less than a metre wide; they could be crossed in a stride. If there was any further reinforcement of this barrier, it was probably little more than a brushwood fence. Separating these long, narrow plots from the Street to their east was a strip of open land some 5 metres wide with a shallow, metre-wide ditch on its western edge. This ditch, equal in length to from two to four house lots, was discontinued in only one place, mid-

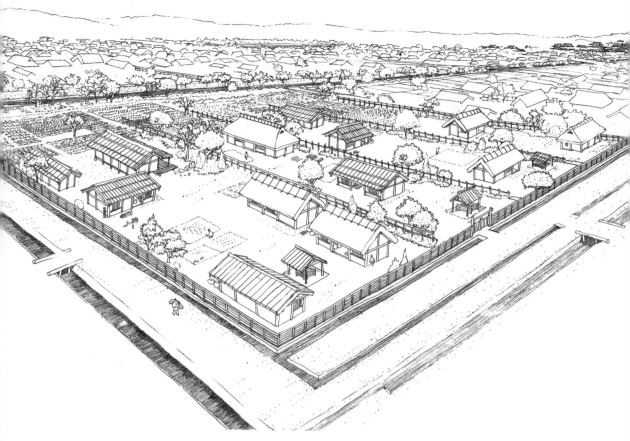

**61** Reconstruction of a residence northeast of the East Market. The further south in Nara Capital one goes, the lower the rank of the residents and the smaller the residential lots and dwellings.

way along its length; the remains of a gate were found at that point. Assuming that this gate provided access through some kind of fence, then the residents of all but one of the lots would have had to step across the narrow east-west ditches and walk through a neighbour's land in order to pass through the gate and reach the Street. To sum up, since each plot had its own well, the neighbours seem to have carried on relatively independent existences; but at the same time, they must have been in a close enough personal relationship to pass freely over each other's land.

Written sources pertaining to the residential situation in Nara Capital are disappointingly scarce. The sole surviving document to shed light on the family composition of Nara residents is a small fragment of the Right Capital tax register of 733. This is a collection of forms filled out by the head of each household. Besides recording the number of members in the household, the register gives personal information on each member: age, sex, appearance, and whether liable for or exempt from taxation (fig. 62). These forms suggest that households in the capital, like those in the agricultural villages, were very large. The Right Capital tax register provides complete data for nine households: their average size is 16.4 members, ranging from 28 down to 9. The membership might include the head couple, their children, parents, unmarried siblings, but also the families of married siblings, certain other dependents, and in some cases a few slaves. Thus a single household could contain

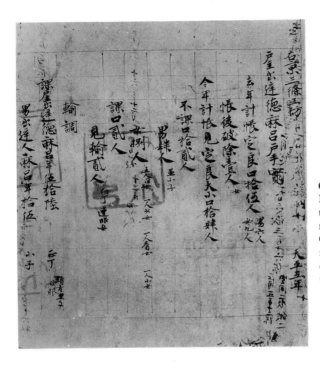

**62**
Fragment of the Right Capital
tax register of A.D. 733. A fragment of a tax register of the Right
Capital survives in the Shōsōin
repository. It provides crucial
clues for estimating the population of Nara Capital.

several nuclear family units as well as some additional personnel. This was the situation on paper—but could all of these people actually have lived together?

The answer may lie in the results of the East Market Northeast Residential
District excavation. It may be that the small lots of 1/8 or 1/16 *chō* were intended for
occupancy by a single nuclear family unit. Several of these together would constitute one of the large households recorded in the tax register. The residents could
move freely across the land of other members of the household, so a single entrance-
way would have sufficed for the entire compound. If one of these lots of 1/16 *chō*
were shared by two families, then each would in effect be living in an area of 1/32
*chō*—as in the case of our money-borrowing lower official. But this might not be
recorded officially as a single house lot of 1/32 *chō*. It is easier to imagine that just
after the establishment of Nara Capital the government allotted a large plot of land
to each of the extended households recorded in the tax register, leaving it, as time
passed, to the members to work out the actual assignment of living areas to each
smaller family unit.

Another interesting document to survive is a copy of a complaint to the government over a question of inheritance of a house and lot. The plaintiff's father
originally lived in Right Capital, 7th Row, 3rd Column and had divided his lot into
two units; after his marriage, the father had acquired an adjoining plot, giving him
finally a total of four units. The father's younger sisters also resided in one or more
of these units. After the father's death, his sisters—our plaintiff's aunts—treated
the entire lot as their own; they refused to yield ownership to their nephew, who
had been living in a separate lot in Left Capital, 7th Row, 1st Column. He now apparently wished to claim the original land as his rightful inheritance. This docu-

ment lends further support to our image, derived from the situation at the East Market Northeast Residential District, of a single large lot being divided into smaller units.

This is as far as we can go for the moment in clarifying the residential patterns of Nara Capital; further conjectures must await the results of future excavations. There is, however, one more interesting fact that has emerged. When Nara Capital was established, the entire area was presumably under state ownership, and the house lots were parceled out according to rank and family size. Subsequently we find house lots being offered as security for loans or becoming the object of inheritance disputes. The public land has become private property.

We have inferred that the North Palace Garden Mansion site (Sub-block 6 in Left Capital, 3rd Row, 2nd Column) had an area of 1 *chō* or more. The largest building in the site had an area of 214 square metres. This was a base-stone building with a tiled roof. The calculation of the building's area is based on the outermost row of pillars. To the northeast of this site, where the City Hall now stands, was Sub-block 15, another lot of 1 *chō*. That lot contained two large structures of 320 and 180 square metres. Both were embedded-pillar buildings and acquired tile roofs during renovations in the latter half of the century.

In Left Capital, 4th Row, 4th Column, where Ō-no-Yasumaro lived, we have established that Sub-block 9 constituted a residential lot of 1/2 or 1 *chō*. The largest building found there so far measures 107 square metres, but only part of the sub-block could be excavated, and the excavator is of the opinion that this building was secondary to an undiscovered larger building. In any case, it was an untiled embedded-pillar structure. Down in the East Market Northeast Residential District, the largest structure found in a lot of 1/8 *chō* was 95 square metres, and the 1/16-*chō* lots have yet to reveal a building exceeding 37 square metres. No roof tiles were found in this district.

The different parts of Nara Capital therefore presented a range of different appearances: to the north, extensive lots containing large-scale buildings worthy of being called palaces or mansions; further south, smaller structures in smaller lots. In the north, after the mid-century at any rate, impressive tile-roof edifices struck the eye everywhere, while in the south, the houses apparently continued to wear their hats of wood, bark, or thatch. Even among tile-roofed buildings, there was quite a disparity between the Palace and the surrounding area of the capital. If we use eave tiles as a measure (making certain assumptions about the actual number of tiles used), the proportion of eave tiles which bore patterns was much higher within the palace grounds. In the central part of the palace grounds, excavation of an area of 1 are (100 square metres) yields an average of 15 to 30 patterned tiles. Outside the grounds, the highest figure is 5; even the North Palace Garden Mansion site turned up only two patterned tiles.

Another factor affecting the urban landscape is the ratio of total land area to the area actually occupied by buildings—the percentage of built-up land. Due to frequent rebuilding, these figures change over time, but a rough calculation based on excavation data gives suggestive results. At the North Palace Garden Mansion site, only 8 to 10 per cent of the land surface was built up—but remember that this was an ornamental garden. To the northeast, in Sub-block 15 of 3rd Row, 2nd Column, the figure stood at 17 per cent during the first half of the century but fell back to 9 per cent thereafter. In Sub-block 9 of Left Capital, 4th Row, 4th Column, the figures varied from 14 to 24 per cent. Further to the south, in the lower-status East Market Northeast Residential District, the built-up rate was a mere 6 to 7 per cent—quite unthinkable to a modern Japanese. Thus the density of building was considerably higher in the neighbourhoods occupied by higher-ranking officials. Incidentally, according to the stipulations of present-day zoning codes, in modern Japanese cities the built-up rate should be less than 80 per cent, and in suburban residential districts no more than 60 per cent.

Along with the modern-day reconstructed garden on the site of the North Palace Garden Mansion, an embedded-pillar building has also been reconstructed. It stands nearly 8 metres tall and its pillars are 40 centimetres thick (see fig. 58, pl. 4 *bottom*). In contrast, the buildings in the East Market Northeast Residential District seem to have been no more than 4 to 5 metres tall, and a pillar as large as 20 centimetres was exceptional. These were puny, shabby buildings when compared with the magnificent structures of the north; and they were scattered very thinly over the land. Perhaps there were vegetable gardens in between these buildings. These southern house lots were not surrounded by towering walls that hid them from view as in the north, although there were earthen walls separating them from the Avenues. Along the Streets that demarcated the sub-blocks, however, the barriers were nothing more than flimsy board or brushwood fences. No doubt one could catch a glimpse of one's neighbours working in their gardens. This certainly is not our typical modern urban landscape; in fact, it was little different from the nearby farming villages. It should nevertheless be remembered that the people of eastern Japan were still living in pit-houses at this time.

Measuring within its outermost line of pillars, the embedded-pillar building which has been rebuilt in the revived North Palace Garden Mansion has an area of 106.2 square metres. The direct expenses of reconstructing this building totalled ¥118,500,000—an average of ¥1,115,000 per square metre. If we use this figure to predict the cost of reconstructing the buildings in Sub-block 15 at the City Hall site (see fig. 60)—not including walls, wells, any unexcavated buildings, and other peripherals, but only those buildings already discovered—the total comes to the astronomical sum of ¥900,000,000. At the present time, to build a Nara period mansion with all its attendant facilities on a lot of 1 *chō*, assuming that the land could be obtained free of charge, would require an outlay in excess of ¥1,000,000,000. In September 1990, this was equivalent to U.S.$7,200,000.

### Daily lives of the capital's residents

Let us assume that Ō-no-Yasumaro did indeed reside in Left Capital, 4th Row, 4th Column as his memorial plaque states. This block (see fig. 54) was enclosed by four Avenues: 3rd Row Avenue to the north, 4th Row Avenue to the south, East 3rd Column Avenue to the west, and East 4th Column Avenue to the east. Like other blocks, this one was sliced into sixteen sub-blocks by six intersecting Streets. We have no idea which sub-block Yasumaro lived in, but let us imagine him on his way to work in the palace each morning. The shortest route would presumably take him through a gate into 3rd Row Avenue. Proceeding westward, he would come to a large intersection every 530 metres or so (1,500 large *shaku*), crossing East 3rd, 2nd, and 1st Column Avenues in succession. A bridge would lead across the ditch on either side of each road. If the Avenue was some 25 metres wide, then we might imagine the bridge as being about half that width. Turning north at East 1st Column Avenue, Yasumaro would see the palace in the distance. After another 530 metres he would come to the intersection with 2nd Row Avenue. From this point, continuing northward for another 260 metres would bring him to the palace's Chiisako Gate, straddling East 1st Column Avenue; if he turned left instead and walked 260 metres to the west, he would find Mibu Gate on his right. Assuming that Yasumaro was first required to appear at the State Halls Compound for the Morning Obeisance, Mibu Gate would probably have been more convenient. In all, Yasumaro would have walked a little more than 2 kilometres.

Now imagine Mr. X, a low-ranking functionary living in the East Market Northeast Residential District, in Sub-block 9 of Left Capital, 8th Row, 3rd Column. Turning north on the Street to the east of his house, he comes to 7th Row Avenue. Turning left, he quickly encounters East Horikawa River, perhaps 10 metres wide and 2 metres deep. Some 800 metres to the south of this point, where one of the Streets crossed this river, excavation has revealed a bridge 3 metres wide (fig. 63); the bridge here on the Avenue was doubtless much wider. The bridge piles in the excavated example were sharpened logs, 30 to 50 centimetres in diameter, which supported crossbeams to hold the board planks. The piles and crossbeams were joined by mortise and tenon, but the floor planks as well as the side walls of the bridge surface seem to have been held in place with ropes rather than the more usual nails. It has been suggested that this was to facilitate the dismantling of the bridge in times of flooding. The bridge surface seems to have been paved over with earth. Anyhow, Mr. X's daily walk to the palace gate would cover some 4 kilometres, about twice the distance of Yasumaro's.

At a certain time each day, varying with the season, a drum would sound and the Outer Great Wall Gates would be opened. The Engi Shiki collection of procedures divides the year into forty periods, each with its specific opening time. For example, from late December to early January the gates were to open shortly after 6:30 A.M., but in late June they would open at 4:30 A.M. About an hour later, the gates to the State Halls Compound and various offices and bureaux were also opened. Failure to report on time on assigned work days would affect one's work record adversely. Those lower officials who had no horse would have to set out from home as early as 4:00 A.M. in the summer. Regardless of the season, however, the officials' workday came to an end exactly four hours after the office gates had opened. They would be free by 9:30 A.M. in mid-summer! The closing time for the Outer Gates also varied seasonally, being set at shortly after 5:00 P.M. in late December but at around 7:30 P.M. in late June. These opening and closing times were of course linked with the movements of the sun: the gate-opening drum would be heard about 18 minutes (in modern terms) before sunrise, and the gate-closing drum sounded 18 minutes after sunset (fig. 64). Like modern workers, Nara officials had to report at a certain time and work a certain number of hours; the difference is

**63** Bridge over the East Horikawa River. At Nara Capital, channeled rivers 10 m wide flowed south through the Left and Right Capitals. These were of great use in the transport of goods.

that the reporting time was not always the same. Even in an urban setting, these ancient office workers, just like the farmers in the surrounding villages, found their daily lives tuned to the rhythms of nature. In that respect, life for the early Japanese town-dwellers had a totally different quality from that of their modern urban counterparts.

The farmer rises with the dawn and retires at sundown; what about our officials? After dark, oil lamps were used to provide light. These were simply tableware vessels which had been filled with oil. Large numbers of such lamps have been excavated from Nara Palace and from the temples of the capital, but very few have been found in residential areas. At Heian Capital, lamps were to become a standard household item, but the citizens of Nara seem to have spent the hours of darkness in sleeping.

A small number of these lamps have provided some very interesting data. Until recently it was assumed that all organic matter decayed underground and vanished without trace, but it has been found that tiny quantities of certain fats, especially fatty acid and sterol, may survive in a relatively stable form. Thus some oil lamp sherds preserve traces of the fuel that they once held. From this evidence we know that the lamps of the Nara period burned oil from rape seed or fish and beef suet. Research utilizing such fatty residues has developed rapidly in Japan over the last ten years or so, and has been applied to soil examination as well as to artifacts of

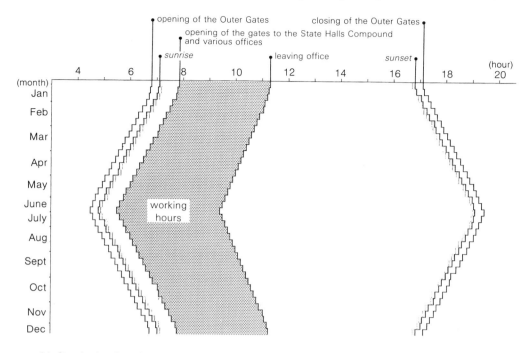

**64** Graph showing the opening and closing times of Nara Palace gates and the bureaucrats' arrival and departure times throughout the year. Sunrise and sunset provided the standard for the working hours of the bureaucrats and the opening and closing of the gates. Though urban residents, they lived a daily cycle similar to the farming populace.

virtually all materials, reaching well back into the prehistoric period. It has been possible, for example, to determine that a certain pit had been used as a grave, or to tell exactly what was cut with a particular stone knife, what was cooked in a particular pot, what animal's bone was used to make a particular object—the results are varied and impressive.

Let us next consider what is known of the diet of the citizens of Nara. Rice had already become the staple diet of the Japanese by this period; then as now, other dishes were secondary. Seafoods—fish, shellfish, seaweed—were the principal side dishes. Venison and wild boar meat were less common than in earlier eras but continued to be eaten. Domesticated animals, however, furnished virtually no food, except for a small quantity of dairy products which were apparently considered to be medicinal or nutritional supplements. Evidence for the range of foods stems both from documentary sources and from large numbers of wooden tablets. It is interesting that chopsticks, which were quite rare at Fujiwara Palace, had become abundant at Nara Palace. They seem to have been used regularly at palace meals and banquets. Outside the palace, though, they were still uncommon. It is only in the Heian period that chopsticks came to be used by the majority of citizens.

How many officials were at work in Nara Palace? Naoki Kōjirō, Professor Emeritus of Osaka City University, has calculated the total number of employees in the offices of the central government as 6,487. This does not include the women who served in the Imperial Domicile, nor the assistants to the higher nobles and officials. The overall total might well have surpassed 10,000. Not that they all came to the palace every day. The vast majority of officials were from the lower ranks and might work only two or three days a week. The total work population on a given day was probably a few thousand. However, not all of these officials resided in Nara for the whole of each year.

Evidence for this is provided by a very interesting *mokkan* (fig. 65). It bears the names of nine officials, six on the front and three on the back. Their offices are not specified, but because of urgent business, they are being ordered to appear for work at the palace on a day on which they are not normally scheduled to do so. Six of their names are accompanied by the names of counties within Yamato Province, one of which lies some 30 kilometres from Nara Palace. The tablet also states that the food and horses necessary for the trip will be provided. It thus appears that six of the nine officials were living outside the capital and came to Nara only on workdays. The other three presumably resided in the capital.

Nabunken's Kitō Kiyoaki has been studying the work-evaluation tablets concerning the lower-ranking officials, described in Chapter 3 (pp. 79–81). Of 215 workers whose registered domicile is recorded, only 15 per cent were listed as residents of Nara Capital, and another 14 per cent were registered elsewhere in Yamato Province. Thirty-seven per cent were registered in provinces adjacent to Yamato, and the remaining third were scattered from the northern tip of Honshū to Kyūshū in the south. The 85 per cent who were not registered in Nara Capital seem to have been sent or called to the capital for a limited stay, whether alone or with a family. Then they would eventually return to their homes elsewhere in the country. Many of the people residing in the capital at a given moment would have been temporary residents of this kind.

According to one estimate, the population of Nara Capital was about 200,000, including the nobility and such temporary residents, while Japan as a whole had five to six million inhabitants. These figures appeared in 1927 in Sawada Goichi's *Statistical Research on the Civil Economy of the Nara Period*. Born in 1861 in what is now Gifu Prefecture, Sawada put himself through school, graduating in 1891 from the Physics Department of Tokyo Imperial University. After various teaching jobs, he was appointed in 1897 to a professorship at Tokyo Higher Commercial School (present-day Hitotsubashi University). His teaching and numerous publications dealt particularly with economics and mathematics. Retiring at the age of sixty, he re-enrolled as a student at Tokyo Imperial University—this time in the Japanese History Department. His doctoral dissertation was reworked for a general readership, resulting in the book mentioned above. Sawada died in 1931, four years after its publication. Later researchers on population and other statistical aspects of the Nara period have taken Sawada's work as a point of departure.

Sawada based his calculations on documentary evidence, and a document which sheds some light on the accuracy of his national population figure has recently been discovered. It was among a number of documents, recovered from the Kanoko-C site in Ibaragi Prefecture, which were fortuitously preserved when the paper became impregnated with japan-lacquer. Kanoko-C was the site of an administrative facil-

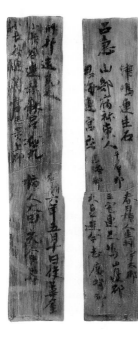

**65**
Wooden tablet ordering officials to come to work. From this *mokkan* we can see that many lower-ranking officials employed at Nara Palace lived in farming villages outside the capital.

ity not far from the main government offices of Hitachi Province; it was in use from the late eighth to early ninth century. A rescue excavation was conducted at the site between 1979 and 1982, prior to construction of the Jōban Highway. A total of 3,857 fragments of lacquer-coated paper documents were recovered. These documents had not been intentionally lacquered. It appears that they had been used to keep lacquer itself from hardening, by serving as a lid for a bowl of lacquer or by being laid directly on the surface of the lacquer to provide an air seal. In the course of time, the paper absorbed some of the lacquer. The lacquered segments were highly resistant to decomposition during centuries of burial. Examples of this type have been found at Nara Palace as well.

In most cases the colour of the lacquered sections has changed to a rich brown, so that any writing in China ink might go unnoticed by the naked eye. Infrared television provides the solution to the problem. An infrared camera records the amount of thermic (i.e., infrared) radiation reflected from the object. When the amount is high, the screen shows white; when low, the screen shows black. In the case of lacquered paper, the carbonic component in the ink absorbs almost all of the thermal rays, but the rest of the surface is highly reflective. Thus the written message stands out clearly in black on the screen (fig. 66).

An infrared study of the Kanoko-C paper fragments revealed that almost all of them were originally documents pertaining to official business. When no longer needed for official purposes, they were consigned to use as lacquer covers—fortunately for us. Among these is one fragment which contains what appears to be a figure giving the total population of Hitachi Province subject to central governmental control. It allows us to conjecture that the province's total population was approximately 200,000. The figure published by Sawada Goichi early in 1927, on the basis of a survey of available data, was 216,900. With such striking confirmation of this particular case, Sawada's figure of five to six million for the whole of Japan gains considerably in credibility.

Using the same methods that proved so successful in predicting the population of Hitachi, Sawada arrived at a figure of 200,000 for Nara Capital. He admitted, however, a potential margin of error of from 20,000 to 50,000. Since then, his figure of 200,000 has been treated as the standard. It is only recently that another hypothesis has been offered: Kishi Toshio's figure of 100,000. In going over Sawada's sources and calculations, Kishi, Professor Emeritus of Kyoto University, felt dubious about certain of Sawada's assumptions. He was therefore moved to attempt his own calculation. He started with a passage in the entry for the eleventh month of the first year of Keiun (704) in the *Shoku Nihongi* chronicle. In connection with the establishment of Fujiwara Capital, the passage says, residents were given rolls of cloth. It is clear that the number of recipient households was 1,505. Kishi is of the opinion that this represents the total number of households in Fujiwara Capital. If Fujiwara Capital had 1,505 households, then Nara Capital, with a total area more than three times that of Fujiwara, must have had at least 4,500 households. We noted earlier that a surviving fragment from the tax register of Right Capital (for the year 733) yields an average household size of 16.4 members (p. 119). Multiplying this by 4,500, one gets a figure of about 74,000. Assuming that the number of households increased during the years of the Nara period, Kishi offers a final estimate of about 100,000 residents.

Calculations of this sort, of course, are really 'guesstimates', with assumptions piled upon assumptions, making them difficult to evaluate without further data from the archaeological record. Any new proposal would be equally hard to judge. We shall, however, offer a different viewpoint on the matter, which will allow us to express a tentative preference for one of the two existing hypotheses.

Earlier in this chapter (pp. 103–7), we accepted the assumption that the specifications for house lot distributions contained in an imperial edict from Fujiwara Capital were potentially valid guidelines to the situation at Nara Capital. One section stipulated that lower-rank officials or citizens of no rank would receive land according to household size: large households, 1 *chō;* medium-size, 1/2 *chō;* small, 1/4 *chō.* Another document equated these three categories of household size with the number of adolescent or adult male members: a minimum of eight, four, and two respectively. Notice that the ratio of these three figures (8:4:2, i.e., 4:2:1) is the same as the ratio of corresponding house lot sizes. For each adolescent or adult male, an area of 1/8 *chō* or somewhat less was to be provided. Going back once again to the fragmentary Right Capital tax register, we find that the average size of a family unit including only one adult male would have been 6.7. The Fujiwara edict specifies a plot of 1 *chō* for a household with eight *or more* males; multiplying 8 by 6.7, we can hypothesize that a *minimum* average of 53.6 people shared a single *chō* of land.

If we next set aside some uncertainties about the exact size of Nara Capital and tentatively accept the majority view, then the capital contained 1,368 *chō.* From this we subtract 76 *chō* for Nara Palace and approximately 150 *chō* covered by temples, markets, rivers, mounded tombs, and so forth; that leaves slightly less than 1,150

**66** Reading lacquered inscriptions with infrared television. When sheets of paper were used to seal lacquer-storage containers, the lacquer often adhered to the paper, preventing its decay and preserving it to the present day. Many of these sheets were inscribed with characters in ink. These characters are difficult to read with the naked eye (*left*), but can be deciphered using infrared television (*right*).

*chō* of land for housing. If we now multiply this by our minimum average population for a 1-*chō* plot, we get 62,000. All of this is of course based on the Fujiwara edict's *minimum* figures for household size; a household of no rank with many more than eight males would still only receive 1 *chō* of land. If we assume that there were indeed many more than the minimum number of males as population increased, then the same amount of land might eventually have held 50 per cent more people, giving a total population figure of almost 100,000. Now we must add in the monks, priests, and other people residing in the capital's temples; their number has been put at over 10,000. But we must also consider that there is a hilly region in the western part of the capital (see fig. 2) which may not have been as densely settled as the rest; and we may also safely assume that the northern half of the capital, the district of nobles and high-ranking officials, was much more sparsely populated than the south. Thus we must subtract an unspecified number from our population figure. Obviously we cannot arrive at a very precise final estimate, but we can suggest that Sawada's figure of 200,000 is highly unlikely. Kishi's 100,000 seems to be an absolute maximum.

## Cities of Japan, cities of the world

In the seventh century the first centralized Japanese state established its base in the Asuka region of southern Yamato and ruled the entire land from there. The headquarters of this polity was a palace district of a few hectares, containing the emperor's living quarters (later called the Imperial Domicile) and the offices of the highest executive organs of government (corresponding to the later State Halls Compound and Great Supreme Hall). This palace was relocated several times within the Asuka district. During this process, additional administrative offices gradually accumulated around the palace, as the functions of the central government were elaborated. These offices too were eventually absorbed into the palace grounds, which expanded to a few dozen hectares in area. Here we have the prototype of Nara Palace. At the end of the century, this centre of government evolved into a fully fledged capital city, with a layout based on the Chinese system: a regular grid of streets spreading out symmetrically from the palace. The first such capital was established at Fujiwara in 694 and had an area of nearly 600 hectares including the palace. A brief sixteen years later, a new capital more than three times this size was constructed at Nara. This process of growth culminating in Nara Capital reflects clearly the way in which the ancient Japanese state came to maturity.

Fujiwara, Nara, and Japan's other ancient capitals differ in one important respect from other cities of the ancient world: there were almost no provisions for defence from outside attack. In China and other countries in Asia, as well as in Europe, cities generally grew out of the need for defence. Imposing barriers were erected, and people came to live within their sheltering embrace. If such a barrier had enclosed Nara Capital, it would certainly have come to light by now. But archaeological investigations around the capital's main gate—at the southern end of Scarlet Phoenix Avenue—suggest no more than the possible existence of a simple mud wall. There is absolutely no evidence, at any of Japan's ancient capitals, of the type of mammoth defence walls found in other countries. The lack of concern with self-defence is also reflected in the paucity of military forces. The garrison at Nara Capital consisted of at most 2,000 soldiers. At about the same time at the Chinese capital of Zhang-an, there were 100,000 troops among a population of about a million. All of the ancient Japanese cities shared this demilitarized nature. It must be assumed that the ancient Japanese rulers, although no strangers to internal power struggles within the ruling class, did not perceive any threat of invasion from outside. It was not until the war-torn period between the thirteenth and sixteenth centuries that Japanese cities were girdled with defensive walls.

With a population of less than 100,000, Nara Capital was ancient Japan's largest city. To find a city greater than their own, the residents of Nara would have had to travel abroad. The best opportunity for such a valuable experience was as a member of one of the missions to Tang China. Perhaps two thousand people had this chance during the Nara period. Crossing to the Yangtse delta, they would have seen cities such as Suzhou and Yangzhou with populations of perhaps a few hundred thousand. But no more than two or three hundred of the voyagers would have had the privilege of continuing on to Zhang-an, the capital and largest city within a realm of fifty million people (not including slaves). Zhang-an at that time had a population of a million people living in an area some four times that of Nara Capital. Its population density was about triple that of Nara Capital.

The visitors from the Japanese capital must have been astounded and humbled by the prosperity of Zhang-an. But had they heard of the great cities even further west—of the capital of the Saracens, who had prevailed against the military might of the Tang on the banks of the Talas; of Damascus, seat of the Omayyad empire; of Baghdad, capital of the Abbasid caliphs? Had they heard of Constantinople, capital of the Byzantine empire, whose walls had withstood the Islamic assault on Europe?

Baghdad was built on the banks of the Tigris in the middle of the eighth century. At its heart lay a royal castle whose walls extended for 6.4 kilometres. Its population may have been over a million; some say two million. High-walled Constantinople, at the meeting point of Asia and Europe, is said to have had six hundred thousand to a million people. These two cities ranked with Zhang-an as the largest of their time.

Further to the west, in Europe, the glorious days of the great classical civilizations were long past. Rome, once the capital of a mighty empire, was now relegated to the leadership of a small religious state in central Italy, its people dwelling among the ruins of the golden age. The decline had been equally great among the former strategic outposts of the Roman Empire. London, for example, was now no more than an oversized village of a hundred hectares, with little to hint of its more impressive past or future. But the citizens of Nara Capital had never heard of these places.

# Chapter 5

# Priests, Townsfolk, and Cityfolk

### From Nara Capital to a town of temples and shrines

In 784 Emperor Kanmu moved the capital from Nara to Nagaoka; then a mere ten years later, in 794, he relocated the capital once more in Heian (modern Kyoto). Since the establishment of a centralized government in Japan, the centre of power had rotated exclusively within Yamato Province. With these two moves, the ancient capital left Yamato for the first time, never to return.

Both Nagaoka and Heian Capitals were in Yamashiro Province. Why did Kanmu move the capital from Yamato to Yamashiro? Historians have offered various interpretations. The Nara period, especially its latter half, saw rampant political confusion due to frequent power struggles within the ruling class, combined with extremely strong Buddhist influence over affairs of state. There were also numerous scandals involving officials dispatched by the central government to administer the provinces. In general, state authority seemed in jeopardy.

Furthermore, there was widespread social unrest due to the collapse of the basic principles that had supported the state. The archaic state with the emperor at its centre had as its basic principle that all land and people belonged to the state— 'public land, public people'. In the Nara period, however, to encourage the creation of new arable, a policy was established recognizing private ownership of newly reclaimed lands. Increasingly, moreover, lands that had been given to nobles and officials in association with their positions and ranks did not revert to the state but were privatized and made inheritable. Thus the principle of 'public land, public people' gradually faded away.

Drawing its strength from the privatization of agricultural land, a new landed gentry (*gōzoku*) class was born, among whom descendants of continental immigrants were not uncommon. This newly emergent gentry collided with the traditional power-holders who had worked for the establishment of an emperor-centred state. Kanmu himself was descended from continental immigrants on his mother's side, placing him in a slightly ambiguous position in this regard. Wielding power autocratically, he sought a way to rebuild the shaky ruling structure. Essential to this effort was the relocation of the capital.

After the shift to Yamashiro Province, one drama remained to be played out with the old Nara Capital as its stage. Kanmu died in 806 and was succeeded by his son Heizei. A mere four years later, Heizei abdicated in favour of his younger brother Saga. However, Heizei and his aristocratic backers continued to meddle in the affairs of government, leading to a power struggle between the two brothers' factions. In 810 Heizei's clique plotted to regain power and shift the capital back to Nara. The coup attempt was quickly quashed by Saga's forces; its leaders were executed or committed suicide, and the retired Emperor Heizei was confined to a building on the former Nara Palace site until his death in 824. Traces of this retirement palace were found during excavation (see p. 98).

Despite this brief interlude, the old capital of Nara changed rapidly after its abandonment. According to a source from as early as 864, 'the buildings and streets of Nara Capital have reverted to fields.' Nara and the other early capitals were not cities that grew spontaneously as people gathered out of economic and social necessity, thereby leading to the development of urban institutions: they were aritificial constructs, born of political need. When the political climate shifted, there was no reason for people to stay on in the abandoned capitals. The populace would move to the new capital; the major official buildings would be dismantled and reassembled at the new site; almost nothing remained. Nara was no exception.

But even after the administrative buildings were removed, many temples and shrines still stood among the paddies and fields of Nara. Six state-supported Buddhist temples had been established in Nara: Yakushiji (figs. 67, 68), Daianji, Gangōji, Kōfukuji, Tōdaiji, and Saidaiji. These together with Hōryūji temple, further to the south in Yamato Province, came to be known as the Seven Great Temples of the Southern Capital. The Southern Capital was of course Nara, seen from the perspective of the new Heian Capital—which in turn came to be called Kyōto, 'capital city'. The Nara temples, with their extensive proprietary estates, continued to enjoy official status even after the shift to the north, so the old capital managed to maintain its position as the centre of Japanese Buddhism for a while. Gradually, however, new temples sprang up in and around Heian, and the Seven Great Temples saw their influence decline. The status of state-sponsored temple became a mere formality. Only two of the southern temples managed to keep and extend their power: Tōdaiji, which enjoyed the protection of the imperial family, and Kōfukuji, the clan temple of the influential Fujiwara family. The Fujiwara were already the most powerful of noble families during the Nara period, and they continued to wield influence during the Heian period through their role of providing wives to the imperial family. Not only did both of these temples receive frequent donations of land, contributing to their economic base, but many of the younger sons of the Heian nobility became priests in these temples, further strengthening their bonds with the ruling class. Kōfukuji in particular extended its might during the eleventh century, until it controlled most of the land in Yamato Province. The designation Southern Capital eventually became virtually synonymous with Kōfukuji. To maintain their power, these temples established armies—the so-called warrior-priests. These warrior-priests did more than merely defend the independence of their temples. When the government ignored their wishes, they would even organize demonstrations and march on Heian Palace, wreaking havoc in the capital. In this period, the power of the Southern Capital resided in its warrior-priests.

Meanwhile, during the eleventh century, regional gentry who had broken away from the control of the state and the nobles gradually occupied ever more land until they had effectively become local feudal lords. Arming themselves for defence, they also maintained order in their domains. Forming large clan-like units, they extended their power even further. These were the newly emergent samurai families, and they came into direct confrontation with the power of the warrior-priests of the Southern Capital. Eventually some of the samurai were brought to the capital to serve as guards for the royal and noble houses. Before long, however, they began to wield influence in the resolution of disputes among the nobility, thus acquiring the leverage to become the *de facto* rulers. The first samurai group to grasp power in this way, during the late twelfth century, was the Taira clan—the Heike. The Taira were even able to extend their power into Yamato, among the lands belonging to Kōfukuji. Before long, many Yamato samurai families cut their ties with the great temple and threw in their lot with the Heike.

The Heike were opposed by another powerful samurai group, the Genji or Minamoto clan. Eventually, in 1180, the struggle for supremacy between the Genji and the Heike turned into open warfare. Seeing their chance, the warrior-priests of the Southern Capital launched a counter-attack against the Heike. The Heike dispatched troops to suppress the uprising. At Narazaka—Nara Hill—at the northern entrance into the Southern Capital from Yamashiro Province, forty thousand mounted Heike soldiers routed the seven thousand warriors of Tōdaiji and Kōfukuji. It was the twenty-eighth day of the last month of the year. Still spoiling for battle, the victorious Heike surged down into the former capital and set it aflame. Its temples and shrines were reduced to ashes.

The Heike succeeded in their campaign in Nara, but in the end they suffered a total defeat at the hands of their arch-rivals the Genji.* The Heike had chosen to keep their power base in the imperial capital at Heian—where the seductive influence of aristocratic culture gradually sapped their military might. Learning from this, the Genji established a new military capital some 450 kilometres to the northeast, in Kamakura, west of modern Tokyo. There, far from the pernicious court culture, they were among like-minded warrior friends; from there, through the agency of their local samurai allies, they extended their hegemony over all Japan. So began the Kamakura period, whose dates are usually given as 1185–1333.

The Southern Capital had been left in ruins by the Heike. Its temples and shrines, however, made a rapid comeback. By the end of the twelfth century, not twenty years after their destruction, Tōdaiji and Kōfukuji had been nearly completely rebuilt. The reconstruction process was helped along by the presence of artisans from the Song dynasty, who introduced the latest Chinese architectural technology. The Buddhist statuary and other temple trappings similarly benefited from the adoption of new techniques of manufacture.

Not only had technology changed, but Buddhism itself was undergoing a striking evolution. During the period when the capital rotated within Yamato, Buddhism had been no more than a religion for praying for the protection of the state; in the Heian period, it became a vehicle for the nobility, who would engage priests to

---

*The Genji-Heike wars are described in detail in the epic, *The Tale of the Heike*, and have provided the plots for myriad Kabuki, Noh, and Bunraku plays.

**67** Yakushiji temple. There are still numerous fields in the vicinity of Yakushiji temple, which is located in the old Right Capital of Nara.

**68** Yakushiji temple, showing the excavation area in front of the East Pagoda (eighth century) and the Main Worship Hall (recent reconstruction) behind it.

intercede on personal matters through prayer. Buddhism was now in the process of becoming a religion of the masses. Through the power of personal prayer, both rich and poor could be guaranteed salvation in the next world. With such spiritual and technological developments, the curtain rose on a new era for Japan.

The new religion attracted widespread popular support. Mass pilgrimages to the temples of the Southern Capital became common. New lodgings had to be built for the visitors, and other services provided. Moreover, the concentration of artisans who had gathered to rebuild the temples led to a rebirth of industry. Residential areas grew up around the temples, and by the thirteenth century a new market was founded. These new developments, however, all took place on land controlled by the temples: an independent town had not yet emerged. For even during the samurai-dominated Kamakura period, the governance of Yamato Province was entrusted to Kōfukuji, and each temple still held sway over its own territory. Moreover, these new urban activities were confined basically to the Outer Capital region of old Nara Capital.

In 1333 the Kamakura government toppled, victim of internal power struggles, constant resistance from the nobility of the distant imperial court, and rebellions by local military lords. From then until the sixteenth century the country was tossed in the turmoil of civil instability, as local lords extended their power at the expense of a weakened and divided central government, and popular uprisings became frequent. In Yamato as well, the samurai sought to rid themselves for good of ecclesiastical control, and the people of Nara struggled for similar freedom. Nara was transformed again, from a town of temples and shrines to one of townsfolk.

The decisive point in this process was the Ōnin Disturbance of 1467–77. Kyoto, the centre of the uprising, was reduced to scorched earth, and this became the stimulus for an overturning of the traditional order elsewhere as well. The Nara townsfolk, until then divided into units according to the controlling temple, now formed their own groups to resist the heavy taxation imposed by the monks. The citizenry attempted to take over the administration of the town and the maintenance of order. In reality, they succeeded in escaping ecclesiastic control only to come under the domination of the samurai; self-governance was not yet theirs. In 1559 the powerful warrior Matsunaga Hisahide had a castle built on a hill on the north edge of the town, and from here he governed all of Yamato Province. This was the first time that Nara had come under samurai control. A Jesuit missionary who visited the castle wrote: 'There can be no castle so beautiful in the whole world. . . . The castle gate doors are each made of a single great plank of wood, and the metal-studded pillars look just like pillars of gold. The castle is filled with the fragrance of aromatic wood, and the gardens far surpass those of the [Heian] Capital.'

But these were turbulent times, and Nara could not escape the flames of battle. The Great Buddha Hall of Tōdaiji (cover, fig. 69, pl. 17) burned to the ground—but the people rebuilt it. Under military rule, the townsfolk administered the town. Nara Town emerged and flourished. Until it was overtaken by the international mercantile port town of Sakai in the late fifteenth century, Nara was the second largest town in Japan after Kyoto. Records from the early sixteenth century put its population at 25,000.

**69** Interior of the Great Buddha Hall, Tōdaiji temple. The existing Great Buddha Hall and Great Buddha were reconstructed around the turn of the eighteenth century. They have become focal points for tourists to Nara.

### From Nara Town to Nara City

The task of ending the centuries of warfare and commencing the unification of the country was finally accomplished in the sixteenth century by Oda Nobunaga (1534–82) and his successor Toyotomi Hideyoshi (1536–98). Remarkable among Hideyoshi's policies was the successful separation of military and agricultural roles. He restricted the bearing of arms to the official military and, in his famous 'sword hunt', disarmed the peasantry, thus guaranteeing absolute military rule. Hideyoshi further ordered a survey of all arable land; this provided a basis for direct taxation of individual peasants, allowing the government to eliminate the intermediary role of influential nobility, temples and shrines, powerful samurai, and so forth. With these necessary preliminaries achieved, it was Tokugawa Ieyasu (1542–1616) who took the final step: his victory at the Battle of Sekigahara in 1600 placed the whole country under the control of the Tokugawa shogunate, where it remained in relative peace until 1867. The successive Tokugawa shoguns reigned supreme over the hundreds of local lords (*daimyō*), who in turn governed their fiefs as the principal regional military figures. The Tokugawa government, like the Minamoto regime earlier, chose to avoid the imperial capital and set up headquarters far to the east— in Edo (modern Tokyo). During the Tokugawa period, imperial power gradually withered until the emperor was treated as little more than just another *daimyō*, albeit one deserving of special respect.

The town of Nara had by now escaped entirely from the domination of the temples. The Tokugawas brought Nara under direct shogunal control, responsible not to any local *daimyō* but to a magistrate appointed by the central government. Nara at that time consisted of some 125 wards or neighbourhoods in an area roughly 3 kilometres east to west and 4.5 kilometres north to south, centred on the ancient Outer Capital region (pl. 18). Government of each neighbourhood fell to a committee of influential residents appointed by the magistrate.

Economically, the town was supported by various new industries. Already in the sixteenth century Nara was renowned for its *sake*, ink sticks, swords, fans, charcoal braziers, wooden dolls, etc.; in the next century, linen textiles came to dominate the list. Leading the way was the famous *Nara-zarashi*—linen boiled in a straw ash solution, then pounded in a wooden mortar and bleached in the sun. The result was a snow-white fabric, strong yet soft and graceful. It is said that nine-tenths of the populace derived a living from *Nara-zarashi*. The linen industry peaked in the late seventeenth century, when annual production climbed to over 300,000 rolls (1 roll [*hiki*]=ca. 20 m by 37.5 cm). Incidentally, the population in 1698 was 35,369 divided among 6,123 households—the highest figure since the capital had moved to Nagaoka in the eighth century. By the mid-eighteenth century, however, Nara's textile industry was in terminal decline, battered by competition from other regions, as annual output slumped to a few tens of thousands of rolls towards the end of the Edo period.

The *sake* industry similarly peaked in the mid-seventeenth century and faded thereafter. Annual production at one time reached 16,000 *koku* (1 *koku*=ca. 180 litres), before competition forced a decline.

Manufacture of swords and armour had made the Nara smithies famous during the centuries of warfare, and production continued apace during the still turbulent early decades of the Tokugawa period. Finally, though, peace brought a drastic fall in demand from a peak of some 20,000 swords a year.

Production of ink sticks, fans, and wooden dolls underwent a change in nature in the Edo period, from the status of full-fledged industries to mere souvenir businesses. Popular pilgrimages to the shrines and temples of Nara were then largely a form of amusement and tourism. Indeed, Nara tourist guidebooks were published in profusion from the late seventeenth century onward. Inns numbered 93 at the start of the eighteenth century, and houses of pleasure similarly blossomed. This was the birth of Nara the tourist town. Famous local tourist goods of today, including ink sticks, fans, and Akahada pottery, had their origins in this period. But tourism could not make up for the decline of *Nara-zarashi* and the *sake* industry. By 1857 the population had fallen to 20,661 divided among 4,994 households.

In 1867 the Tokugawa shogunate collapsed; imperial power was 'restored', and the Meiji period (1868–1912) began. The enthusiastic adoption of Western civilization helped Japan join the ranks of modern nation-states. One link in the process was the creation of a new policy of regional administration. The system of provinces and counties, in effect since the seventh century, was replaced by the prefectural system. Yamato Province became Nara Prefecture, and the town of Nara became the prefectural capital.

In this new era, in the world of religion, Shintō gained strength at the expense of Buddhism. Early in the Edo period, as a measure to help eradicate Christian influence, all citizens had been required to register as parishioners of a local temple. As organs of the national power structure, many temples wielded their authority autocratically. Even many Shintō shrines became subsidiary to Buddhist temples. The Meiji government reversed the balance of power, supporting Shintō and confiscating the vast tracts of temple land. The populace at large, after centuries of exploitation by the temples, were only too glad to support the government initiative; in many places, incited by Shintō priests, they destroyed Buddhist buildings and images. Nara did not go unscathed. Even Kōfukuji, once its most powerful temple, was all but deserted as many priests abandoned the cloth. Large numbers of the impressive trees on the temple grounds were felled for firewood; Buddhist ritual objects and texts were sold off; many of the books of sutras were even burned to salvage ornaments of gold and silver. Some of the buildings were used for prefectural offices or a teachers' training school, while some others were sold or simply abandoned. The five-storeyed pagoda (fig. 70) which today stands on the edge of old downtown Nara (pl. 18) is now a valued cultural relic, but in the Meiji period it fell temporarily into other, less respectful hands. The buyer, only interested in the metal fittings, planned to burn down the tower and salvage the metal. His plan was thwarted only because the townsfolk feared the fire would spread.

The life-style of the people of Nara changed in many ways during the Meiji period. To look at developments chronologically, a post office was opened in 1871. Nara's first newspaper was founded in 1872. The first butcher's shops also date from around this time, as the Japanese resumed the eating of meat after centuries of abstinence. The newspaper also carried advertisements for cow's milk. At the Nara Prefectural Office, employees wearing Western clothes kept their shoes on even inside their offices—a shock to a people who had been accustomed to wearing kimono and removing their footwear at the entrance. The first rickshaws also appeared; this method of conveyance continued in use, for tourists at least, until shortly after the Second World War. The year 1873 saw the first police boxes and fire-pumps. Public health advancements included the first vaccinations and, during the 1879 cholera epidemic, the first use of isolation wards away from the town centre. By 1884 watches, electric goods, telephones, and telegraph equipment were being manufactured and sold even in Nara. Modernization had truly begun to affect people's daily lives.

During the Edo period, village and fief schools provided the equivalent of an elementary education to those who were willing and able to attend. In 1872 a modern national system of compulsory public education was launched, derived from Western models; by 1886 Nara had five primary schools. The railroad linked Nara with Osaka in 1890 and with Kyoto in 1896. The first bank dates from 1894. In the same year an electric lighting company was established, and the light of modern civilization shone on Nara.

In 1882 the country's communities were officially classified according to the city-town-village system: Nara was now Nara-*machi*—Nara Town. The townsfolk had hoped Nara would be designated a city, but a population of at least 30,000 was required, and Nara then held only some 24,000. The population criterion was soon met by absorbing several nearby villages, and in 1898 Nara City was born. The new city quickly provided itself with the necessary urban facilities—water supply system, trash dumps, a crematorium, improved roads, and so forth. However, development of the economic base to sustain this new urban life-style lagged behind. Demand for ink sticks and writing brushes was boosted by national compulsory education, but more modern enterprises were slow to develop. Most of the new textile and metal-working firms were merely subcontractors for companies in Osaka—an insecure existence with little scope for expansion.

Lacking major modern industries, Nara came to rely heavily on tourism. In 1890 tourists spent 115,000 nights in Nara's inns, with foreign visitors accounting for 266 of them. In 1896 the former figure had passed the 120,000 mark, and some 1,120 foreign tourists stayed a total of 301 nights in town. Nara also became a popular destination for the newly launched school study excursions, a form of group travel which has since been a major element in domestic tourism. Nara Park, established in 1880 and renowned for its herd of tame deer, continued to develop; in 1895 the country's third National Museum, after those in Tokyo and Kyoto, was erected within its confines. Such developments did indeed contribute to the growth of tourism. In 1920 the total number of nights' lodgings reached 185,000, with overseas visitors accounting for 1,933 of these.

The air raids of the Second World War bathed most major Japanese cities in flames. Nara's citizens suffered greatly on a personal level during the war, but the city itself escaped direct damage. The postwar period saw the rapid urbanization of the areas around Nara. As these were absorbed into the city, Nara for the first time surpassed the size and scope of its glory days of the eighth century. Not until 1955 did the modern city reach the 100,000 population figure attributed to the ancient Nara Capital. By 1990 the figure stood at 344,000. Many of Nara's citizens,

**70** Five-storeyed pagoda, Kōfukuji temple. Kōfukuji temple, built in the eighth century, has met
with fire on many subsequent occasions, and nothing of the original structure remains. The
five-storeyed pagoda, which dominates the present Nara skyline, was reconstructed in 1426.
Even it was threatened with removal in the late nineteenth century.

however, commute west to Osaka or north to Kyoto for their work. Over half of the adult male working-age population leaves the city each day; the figure for women is about 15 per cent. Of the some 10,000 business concerns in Nara City, more than three-fourths are small service businesses such as restaurants and retail shops; manufacturing and construction firms account for little more than 10 per cent of the total. Modern Nara City is principally a residential suburb dependent on the larger surrounding cities for employment and consumption items.

Nara's future as a tourist centre is by no means bright either. In 1980, 14.5 million tourists visited Nara, staying over for 2.3 million nights, but the figures have stagnated at that level ever since. The one bright spot is that foreign tourists have increased from 70,000 in 1980 to 256,000 in 1989.

Japan's first centralized state was born and developed in Yamato Province— present-day Nara Prefecture. It developed a flourishing culture, absorbing many of the best elements from the more advanced continental civilizations, and reaching its peak while the capital was in what is now Nara City. Many of the splendours of that ancient capital are still to be seen in the modern city. It is the search for the roots of modern Japanese culture that brings many domestic tourists to Nara. The citizens of present-day Nara City recognize that the relics of the eighth century are their most precious resource. They also realize, however, that a city of 344,000 people cannot survive on tourism alone: economic development is an absolute necessity. The demands of such development cannot help but come into conflict at times with the need to preserve a precious cultural heritage. How can Nara guarantee the continuance of the charming life-style of a medium-size city, while also ensuring the survival of a proud past, and still develop to meet the needs of the modern world? This is the question confronting Nara today.

# List of Translation Equivalents

Agency for Cultural Affairs: *Bunkachō*
Avenue: *Ōji*

Banquet of the Meandering Stream: *Kyokusui-no-en*
Base stone: *Soseki*
Board of Education: *Kyōiku Iinkai*
Bureau of Inner Stables: *Naikyū-ryō, Uchi-no-umaya-no-tsukasa*
Bureau of Royal Mews: *Shume-ryō, Shume-no-tsukasa*
Buried Cultural Properties Information Retrieval System: *Maizō Bunkazai Jōhō Katsuyō Shisutemu*

Chamberlain: *Jijū*
Column (in street addresses): *Bō*
Committee on Construction: *Kensetsu Iinkai*
Committee on Culture and Education: *Bunkyō Iinkai*
Committee for the Protection of Cultural Properties (=CPCP): *Bunkazai Hogo Iinkai*
Confessionals: *Keka-dokoro*
*Considerations on Nara Capital and the Greater Palace Enclosure: Heijō-kyō oyobi Daidairi Kō*
County: *Kōri*

Department of Palace Affairs: *Kunaishō*
Divination Bureau: *Onmyō-ryō*
Dragon Tail Platform: *Ryūbidan*

East Domicile: *Tōdai*
East Garden: *Tōen*
East Market: *Higashi Ichi*
East Palace: *Tōgū*
East Precinct: *Tōin*
Embedded pillar: *Hottate-bashira*
Equestrian Bureau: *Uma-no-tsukasa*

Flat jug: *Heihei*

Geographical Survey Institute: *Kokudo Chiri-in*
Great Catering Office: *Daizenshiki*
Great Palace Compound Wall (a.k.a. Great Wall): *Miyagaki, Ōgaki*
Great Supreme Hall (Compound): *Daigokuden(-'in)*

143

Hall of Prosperity and Happiness: *Burakuin*
Heijō Palace Site Research Department: *Heijō Kyūseki Hakkutsu Chōsabu*
Hidden design: *Anmon*
Historic Site: *Shiseki*
Historic Site Cultural Centre: *Shiseki Bunka Sentā*
House of Councillors: *Sangiin*
House of Representatives: *Shūgiin*

Imperial Domicile: *Dairi*
Important Cultural Property: *Jūyō Bunkazai*
Inner Catering Bureau: *Naizen-no-tsukasa*

Jewelled Hall: *Gyokuden*

Korea Government-General Museum: *Chōsen Sōtokufu Hakubutsukan*

Land Survey Department: *Rikuchi Sokuryōbu*
Law for the Preservation of Historic Sites, Places of Scenic Beauty and Natural
    Monuments: *Shiseki Meishō Tennen Kinenbutsu Hozonhō*
Left Capital: *Sakyō*

Main Worship Hall: *Kondō*
Middle Palace: *Chūgū*
Minister of the Right: *Udaijin*
Ministry of Ceremonies: *Shikibushō*
Ministry of Civil Affairs: *Minbushō*
Ministry of Construction: *Kensetsushō*
Ministry of Education: *Monbushō*
Ministry of the Interior: *Naimushō*
Morning Assembly Halls: *Chōshūden*
Morning Dress: *Chōfuku*
Morning Duties: *Chōsei*
Morning Obeisance: *Chōrei*
Morning Visit: *Chōsan*
Mountain Plum Palace: *Yamamomo-no-miya*
Music Bureau: *Gagaku-ryō, Utamai-no-tsukasa*

Nabunken＝Nara National Cultural Properties Research Institute: *Nara Kokuritsu Bunkazai*
    *Kenkyūjo*
Nara Capital: *Heijō-kyō, Nara-no-miyako*
*Nara Imperial Palace: Archaeological Surveys Carried out in 1959–1961: Heijō-kyū Hakkutsu Chōsa*
    *Hōkoku II: Nara Kokuritsu Bunkazai Kenkyūjo Gakuhō*
Nara Palace: *Heijō-kyū, Nara-no-miya*
Nara University of Arts and Science: *Nara Gakugei Daigaku*
Nara University of Education: *Nara Kyōiku Daigaku*
Nara Women's University: *Nara Joshi Daigaku*
North Palace: *Hokugū, Kita-no-miya*
North Palace Garden: *Kita-no-miya Teien*

*Observations on the Remains of the Great Supreme Hall in Nara Palace:* Heijō-kyū Daigokuden Shiseki Kō
Office of Gate Guardians: *Emonfu*
Outer Capital: *Gekyō*

Palace Hall: *Goten*
Prime Minister: *Dajō-daijin*
Province: *Kuni*

Rear Hall: *Kōden*
Ridge-end tile: *Onigawara*
Right Capital: *Ukyō*
Road Bureau: *Dōrokyoku*
Row (in street addresses): *Jō*
Royal Mews: *Shume-ryō, Shume-no-tsukasa*

*Sake* Brewery: *Sakadono*
*Sake*-making Bureau: *Zōshu-shi, Sakezukuri-no-tsukasa*
Scarlet Phoenix: *Suzaku, Sujaku, Shujaku*
Sewing Bureau: *Nuidono*
South Garden: *Nan'en*
Special Historic Site: *Tokubetsu Shiseki*
State Halls Compound: *Chōdōin*
*Statistical Research on the Civil Economy of the Nara Period: Nara-chō Jidai Minsei Keizai no Sūteki Kenkyū*
Street: *Kōji*
Sub-block: *Tsubo*

Tamped-wall corridor: *Tsuiji-kairō*
Tokyo National University of Fine Arts and Music: *Tōkyō Geijutsu Daigaku*
Twelve Halls: *Jūnidōin*

West Buddha Hall: *Nishi-no-Butsuden*
West Market: *Nishi Ichi*

West Palace: *Saigū*
Wooden tablet: *Mokkan*

# Translators' Suggested Readings

'History of Japan: Prehistory, Protohistory' and 'Ritsuryō system' entries in the *Kodansha Encyclopedia of Japan*. Tokyo: Kodansha, 1983.

*Japanese Prehistory*. Special issue of the journal *Asian Perspectives* 19, no. 1 (1978). University of Hawaii Press.

> A collection of generalist papers on the various periods of Japanese prehistory including two on historical archaeology relating to Nara Palace.

Aikens, C. Melvin, and Higuchi Takayasu. 1982. *Prehistory of Japan*. New York: Academic Press.

> A site atlas with brief bridging sections giving a general description of the nature of the Japanese archaeological periods up to, but not including, the Nara period.

Aston, W. G., trans. 1972. *Nihongi, chronicles of Japan from the earliest times to A.D. 697*. Tokyo: Charles E. Tuttle Company.

> A translation of the court history compiled in A.D. 720 just after the establishment of Nara Palace.

Barnes, Gina L. 1988. *Protohistoric Yamato: Archaeology of the first Japanese state*. Ann Arbor: Museum of Anthropology and Center for Japanese Studies, University of Michigan.

> An archaeological investigation into the changes in settlement patterning in Nara during the period of state formation preceding Nara Palace.

Hayashi Ryōichi. 1977. *The Silk Road and the Shosoin*. Heibonsha Survey of Japanese Art 6. Tokyo: Weatherhill.

> A work exploring the continental sources of the treasures in the Shōsōin, the imperial storehouse in use during the occupation of Nara Palace and still surviving today.

Hempel, R. 1983. *The Heian civilization of Japan*. Oxford: Phaidon.

> A cultural history of the florescent Heian court society in the Heian period, after the removal of the palace from Nara to Kyoto.

Inoue Mitsusada. 1977. "The *ritsuryo* system in Japan." *Acta Asiatica* 31:83–112.

> A detailed description of the Chinese-style bureaucratic and legal system forming the basis of Nara Palace rule.

Miller, Richard J. 1978. *Japan's first bureaucracy: A study of eighth-century government*. Ithaca: Cornell University East Asia Papers.

> An intricate exploration of the ranking system used in the Nara court.

Pearson, Richard et al., eds. 1986. *Windows on the Japanese past: Studies in archaeology*. Ann Arbor: Center for Japanese Studies, University of Michigan.

> A large collection of mainly specialist papers on various research topics in Japanese archaeology.

Suzuki Kakichi. 1980. *Early Buddhist architecture in Japan.* Tokyo: Kodansha.

    A descriptive treatise on continental architectural styles introduced with the Buddhist faith prior to and during the Nara period.

Tanaka Migaku. 1984. "The archaeological heritage of Japan." In *Approaches to the archaeological heritage,* edited by Henry Cleere. Cambridge: Cambridge University Press.

    An insider's view of the system of rescue archaeology in Japan today, written by one of the authors of the present book.

Tsuboi Kiyotari, ed. 1987. *Recent archaeological discoveries in Japan.* Paris and Tokyo: UNESCO and Centre for East Asian Cultural Studies.

    An introductory text covering the span of Japanese prehistory to early historic society.

Watanabe Yasutada. 1974. *Shinto art: Ise and Izumo shrines.* Heibonsha Survey of Japanese Art 3. Tokyo: Weatherhill.

    A treatise on the two most famous and very early examples of early native architectural styles for religious buildings, to be contrasted with the Buddhist architecture introduced from the continent.

# Index

**1** The northern portion of Nara Capital and Nara Palace, viewed from the south.

**2** The second Great Supreme Hall and Imperial Domicile, Nara Palace.

**3** Excavation activity in the vicinity of the Imperial Domicile, Nara Palace.

**4** Excavation (*top*) and reconstruction (*bottom*) of the pond at the North Palace Garden Mansion, Nara Capital.

**5** Wooden tablets (*mokkan*) unearthed from Nara Palace.

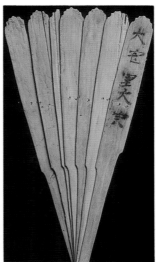

6 *(top)* A ceremonial shield excavated at Nara Palace. *Left:*
original; *right:* reconstructed ver-
sion.

7 *(bottom)* Fan with thin cypress
blades, excavated from a large
mansion in Nara Capital.

**8** Ridge-end tiles excavated at Nara Palace.

**9** Green-glazed bricks (*top*) and eave tiles (*bottom*) from the East Precinct, Nara Palace.

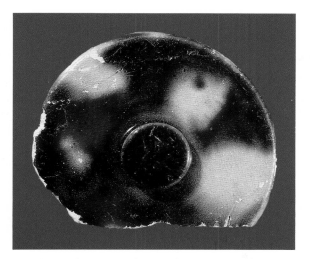

**10** Three-colour ceramic jar lid excavated from Pit SK820, Nara Palace.

**11** Polychrome glazed ceramics excavated from Nara Palace.

**12** Writing tools and samples from the Nara Capital era, including: flat-surfaced *sue*-ware inkstones of different shapes, spouted *sue*-ware water droppers, knife, brush, ink stick, wooden tablets, and part of a Buddhist sutra scroll (replica).

**13** A ram's-head decoration from a ceramic inkstone.

**14** *Haji* vessels used in the ritual exorcism of disease.

**15** Ash-glazed flat jug produced at Sanage kiln near present-day Nagoya City, Aichi Prefecture.

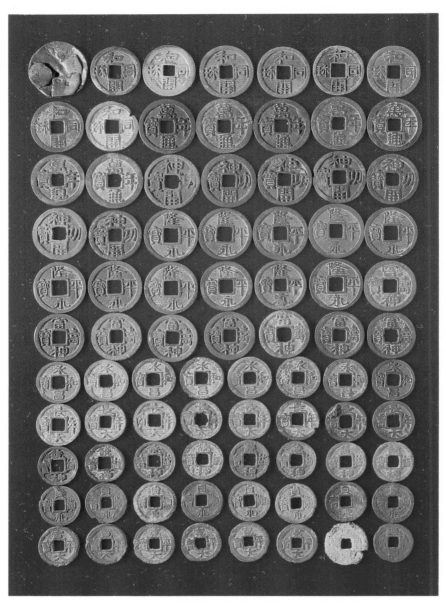

**16** Japanese coins of the seventh to tenth centuries. *Top row left:* seventh-century silver coin; *top row, second and third from left:* Nara-period silver coins; *from top row, fourth coin through fourth row, second coin:* Nara-period copper coins; *remainder:* Heian-period copper coins.

**17** Tōdaiji temple and the northeastern range of mountains of Nara Basin.

**18** The old downtown area of Nara City, which formed the Outer Capital during the Nara
period. Three major temples are visible: Tōdaiji (*upper right*), Kōfukuji (*upper centre*), and
Gangōji (*centre*).

DATE DUE

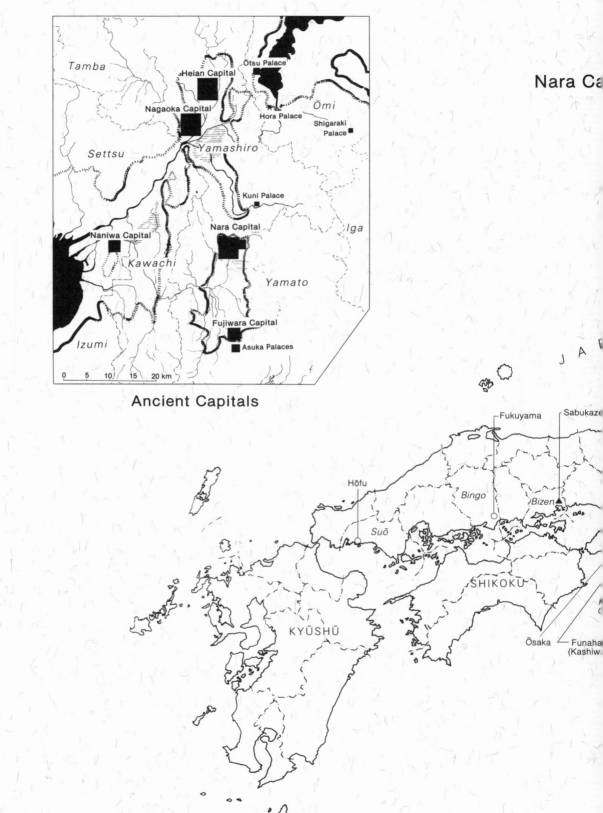

**Ancient Capitals**

Nara Ca

Tamba

Heian Capital

Ōtsu Palace

Nagaoka Capital

Hora Palace

Ōmi

Shigaraki
Palace

Settsu

*Yamashiro*

Kuni Palace

Iga

Nara Capital

Naniwa Capital

Kawachi

Yamato

0   5   10   15   20 km

Fujiwara Capital

Izumi

Asuka Palaces

Fukuyama

Sabukaze

Hōfu

Bingo

Bizen

Suō

J A

SHIKOKU

KYŪSHŪ

Ōsaka

Funaha
(Kashiw